THE VIETNAM WAR: A TEXT FOR STUDENTS

THOMAS WHITTEMORE

Cambridgeport Press • Cambridge, Massachusetts

Library of Congress Cataloging-in-Publication Data

Whittemore, Thomas.
   The Vietnam War: a text for students/Thomas Whittemore
     p. cm.
   Includes index.
   Summary: A high school textbook tracing the history of American involvement in Vietnam from the 1950's to the present day.
   ISBN 0-944348-00-9
   1. Vietnamese Conflict, 1961–1975—United States—Juvenile literature. [1. Vietnamese Conflict, 1961–1975.] I. Title.
DS558.W45 1988
959.704'33'73—dc19
                                                              87-32570
                                                                              CIP
                                                                               AC

Please direct all inquires about this publication to:

Publisher
Cambridgeport Press
15 Chalk Street
Cambridge, MA 02139

About the Author
Thomas Whittemore is an author and editor in the Boston area.

Historical Consultant
Christian G. Appy
Lecturer on History and Literature, Harvard University

Design
Wendy Bedenbaugh

Art Credits
page 30 Michigan State University Archives and Historical Collection **page 50** Department of Defense **page 70** Lyndon Baines Johnson Library **page 90** Lyndon Baines Johnson Library **page 106** Department of Defense **page 130** Department of Defense

Copyright © 1989, 1991 by Cambridgeport Press. All rights reserved.

No part of this work may be reproduced or transmitted in any form or by any means, electronic or mechanical, including photocopying and recording, or by an information storage or retrieval system without prior written permission of the publisher unless such copying is expressly permitted by federal copyright law. Address inquires to Permissions, Cambridgeport Press, 15 Chalk Street, Cambridge, MA 02139.

Printed in the U.S.A.

ISBN: 0-944-34800-9

9 8 7 6 5 4 3

CONTENTS

CHAPTER ONE — THE HISTORY OF VIETNAM TO 1954

1. Vietnam Comes Under French Control 2
2. French Colonial Rule Leaves Its Mark on Vietnam 6
3. The Japanese Occupation Leads to Independence 11
4. The War With France Begins 14
5. The Geneva Peace Conference Divides Vietnam 22

CHAPTER TWO — AMERICA'S GROWING COMMITMENT (1954–1963)

1. Ngo Dinh Diem Leads South Vietnam 32
2. John Kennedy Steps Up American Involvement 38
3. Diem Is Overthrown 44

CHAPTER THREE — THE FIGHTING INTENSIFIES (1963–1967)

1. Lyndon Johnson Tries To Ignore the Situation in Vietnam 52
2. Congress Passes the Gulf of Tonkin Resolution....... 55
3. The United States Becomes Fully Involved in the Vietnam War.................................. 58

CHAPTER FOUR — A DIFFERENT WAR

1. The Vietnam War Is Different From Others Wars 72
2. The War Threatens to Divide the United States 80

CHAPTER FIVE — THE TET OFFENSIVE (1968)

1. The Tet Offensive Stuns the United States and South Vietnam 92
2. More American Troops Are Requested 98
3. Johnson Rejects a Second Term 100

CHAPTER SIX — NIXON AND THE WAR (1969–1973)

1. A New Administration Takes Office and Searches For a Solution to the Vietnam War 108
2. The United States Invades Cambodia 115
3. The War Grinds On 121

CHAPTER SEVEN — WITHDRAWAL AND AFTERMATH (1973 TO THE PRESENT)

1. The United States Withdrawal Leads to a Communist Victory 132
2. Southeast Asia Remains a Region of Turmoil and Confusion 139

KEY DATES IN THE VIETNAM WAR 148
VIETNAM BIOGRAPHY 150
INDEX 155

PROLOGUE

IT WAS 1962, AND TRAVEL AGENTS WERE STILL sending American tour groups to South Vietnam. One traveler, in search of the exotic charms of Saigon, was puzzled. Why, she asked a fellow patron in a restaurant, were there so many Americans in the streets? There was a war going on, she was told, and the United States was involved. "A war?" the tourist answered. "Really? Where?"

Few Americans, like the tourist, had even heard of Vietnam in 1962, let alone its on-going war. Yet, within a few years, Vietnam would hold center stage in the nation's attention. Distant places—Khe Sahn, Hué, Haiphong, Pleiku—would become painfully familiar. Names once unheard-of—Ngo Dinh Diem, Ho Chi Minh, Nguyen Cao Ky, Madame Ngo Dinh Nhu—would be featured on nightly newscasts.

Then, suddenly, it would all be over. By 1973 the last American soldiers had left Vietnam. The nation had lost its first war, and most people wanted to put the whole episode behind them. The nation's attention turned inward—first on Watergate, then on the problems of inflation and oil shortages. Very quickly the names of the people and places that had so long filled the headlines had faded from memory.

Almost a decade after the United States withdrew from the war, the dedication of the Vietnam Veterans Memorial in Washington, D.C., in tribute to the Americans who fought in Vietnam, rekindled interest in the conflict, particularly for a generation that has no memory of it. Questions began to be asked. When did the war start? Who started it? How did the United States become involved? What were we fighting for? What was it like to fight in Vietnam? Why did the war last so long? How did we lose? The answers to those and other questions will be found in this book.

CHAPTER ONE

THE HISTORY OF VIETNAM TO 1954

THROUGHOUT THEIR HISTORY, THE VIETNAMESE people have fought foreign domination. For centuries, China controlled Vietnam. In more recent times, France gained power in much of Southeast Asia. During the years of French control, resistance to colonial rule developed, and Vietnam declared its independence at the end of World War II. France soon returned to Vietnam, however, setting the stage for a long and bitter war, one in which the United States gradually became involved.

In this chapter you will read about the history of Vietnam up to the middle of the 20th century. As you read, look for answers to the following questions:

1. How did Vietnam come under French control?
2. In what ways did French colonial rule leave its mark on Vietnam?
3. How did the Japanese occupation lead to Vietnamese independence?
4. Why was a war fought against France?
5. Why did the Geneva Conference divide Vietnam?

… THE VIETNAM WAR

1 VIETNAM COMES UNDER FRENCH CONTROL

In ancient times, China ruled Vietnam. Even after the Vietnamese formed their own independent state in the mid-900's, Chinese influence remained strong. Then, in the 1600's, European merchants and missionaries began arriving in Vietnam—and with them came a new threat to Vietnamese independence.

The Land and the People Vietnam is a long, narrow country stretching from the borders of China on the north to the delta of the Mekong River in the south. While it may appear small on a world map, Vietnam's area of 130,452 square miles makes it almost as large as the state of California.

Vietnam's shape has often been compared to two rice baskets hanging at the end of a bamboo pole. The baskets are the two major deltas, formed by the Mekong River in the south and the Red River in the north. The Annamese mountain chain, which forms the backbone of central Vietnam, is the pole supporting them.

About 1,000 square miles from north to south, Vietnam is made up of five distinctly different land regions. In the extreme south is the watery world of the **Mekong Delta.** Over half the people of southern Vietnam dwell in the Mekong Delta, living in villages clustered along the sides of irrigation canals and the tributaries of the Mekong River. Travel in this, the chief agricultural region of Vietnam, is almost entirely by boat.

North of the Mekong Delta lie the **central highlands.** Varying in elevation from about 600 feet to over 3,000 feet, this forested region runs through much of western Vietnam. The highlands are sparsely populated by tribes of mountain people.

The rugged peaks of the Annamese (or Truong Son) Mountains—a steep wilderness of dense rain forest, plunging rivers, and tortuous ridges—are found north of the central highlands. These mountains form the **northern highlands** of northwestern Vietnam.

Between the northern highlands and the Gulf of Tonkin is Vietnam's second fertile delta, the **Red River Delta.** Like the Mekong, this region is thickly populated and an important farming area. The two deltas are connected by the **coastal lowlands,** a narrow stretch of land that slopes from the mountains of the central highlands to the South China Sea.

The two deltas and the coastal lowlands, located within the tropics, enjoy warm, moist weather. This climate enables farmers to plant as many as three crops of rice—the nation's main crop—a year.

Chinese Domination Rice was a key to early Vietnam's domination by its mighty neighbor to the north, China. The high yields of rice in the Red River Delta inevitably attracted the attention of the powerful Chinese Empire. So did China's concern about a strong state emerging on its southern border, one which might block Chinese trade with the rest of Southeast Asia.

From 221 B.C. Vietnam began to be brought under Chinese control. As early as 207 B.C., a Chinese general declared himself king of **Nam-Viet** (the Red River Delta area), the first of several such states which were formed over the next 2,000 years. In 111 B.C., the delta region and portions of central Vietnam were conquered by a Chinese army and made a province of imperial China.

During the next 1,000 years, the Vietnamese absorbed many Chinese customs. There was great political restlessness, however, and periodic uprisings and revolts had to be put down·by armies from the north. Then, in 939 A.D., in a successful revolt, the Vietnamese freed themselves of Chinese rule. Except for a brief Chinese occupation (1407–1428), the independent state of **Dai Viet** gained strength. As evidence of China's deep influence in the region, however, Dai Viet's administrative system continued to follow the Chinese model. The Chinese writing system, moreover, was used into the 19th century.

Gia-Long and National Unity By the late 18th century, Vietnam had become a unified state within its present boundaries. The country was given its present name of Vietnam by its emperor, **Gia-Long,** and was ruled from the city of Hué (rather than Hanoi, the principal commercial and administrative city). The brutal Gia-Long, who was assisted by French officers in asserting his control over the country, made great progress in building Vietnamese unity.

Early Contacts with Europe Gia-Long's French advisers were not the first Europeans to arrive in Vietnam. In the 16th century, Portuguese and Spanish traders visited Vietnamese ports; Dutch and English traders followed in the 17th century. That century also marked the arrival of the first French missionaries. Over the years, the missionaries were successful in finding Christian converts. In fact, the Catholic Church had greater success in Vietnam than in any other Asian country apart from the

Philippines (which Spain governed for 400 years). A measure of the missionaries' success is that by the mid-1900's, some 2 million Vietnamese were Christian.

In spite of the missionary presence in Vietnam, for many years French leaders showed little interest in the region. Thoughts of colonizing Vietnam were kept alive, however, by a handful of determined individuals. One such person was Monsignor **Pigneau de Béhaine**, bishop of Adran, who returned to France in 1787, after two decades in Asia. The handsome priest dazzled the French court at Versailles with stories of his adventures. But he was upstaged by a child he had brought back with him, Prince Nguyen Canh. Dressed in red and gold brocade, the seven-year-old pretender to the Vietnamese throne so impressed Queen Marie Antoinette that she bestowed her patronage on the boy, allowing him to play with her son, the heir apparent. Court musicians composed hymns to the exotic youngster, and the queen's personal hairdresser celebrated the visitor by creating a chic new pigtailed coiffure that became the rage at Versailles.

Pigneau's purpose in returning to France was to press for the creation of a Christian empire in Asia. He died before he could arouse much interest in such a scheme, but he played a part in propelling France toward the conquest of Vietnam a century later.

Growing Power of the Missionaries Gia-Long and the Vietnamese emperors who succeeded him, meanwhile, were growing uneasy about the missionaries' presence. They feared the new religion might weaken their authority. More important, they feared that Christianity might be the first step leading to European control—as, indeed, it was. As a result, the Vietnamese emperors gradually tried to withdraw into isolation, turning down proposed pacts with other nations. For instance, **Minh Mang**, successor to Gia-Long, spurned the first American to set foot on Vietnamese soil, Captain John White of Salem, whose clipper ship visited the city of Saigon in 1820. Referring to Westerners as "barbarians," Minh Mang refused to have anything to do with them, pointedly neglecting to establish a department of foreign affairs in his government.

By 1825, Minh Mang decided that the Catholic missionaries in his empire were out of control. Claiming that "the perverse religion of the Europeans corrupts the hearts of men," he banned the entry of any more missionaries into Vietnam. Then, in 1833, suspecting the involvement of missionaries in rebellions against his rule, Minh Mang ordered the arrest of both French and Vietnamese priests. Over the next seven years, ten foreign missionaries were executed, some by slow strangulation.

THE HISTORY OF VIETNAM TO 1954

VIETNAM FACT

One of the first American contacts with Vietnam was made by the **USS Constitution.** *The famous American vessel arrived off the coast of Vietnam in 1845. While in Tourane Harbor (now Danang), its captain, John Percival, received word of a French missionary being held captive in Hué. Eager to help a fellow Westerner, Percival ordered the shelling of the harbor. Nothing came of this gesture, however, and Old Ironsides sailed away.*

France Moves In Reports of cruelties to the missionaries fueled the demand in France to intervene in Vietnam. With the crowning of **Napoleon III** in 1852, French colonialists had at last found official support for their schemes. Both Napoleon and his Spanish wife, Eugénie, were deeply religious and committed to missionary goals in Asia. The new emperor also planned to promote France's national glory through foreign adventures. In this decision, he was following the example of his famous uncle, Napoleon I.

News of the execution of a Spanish missionary in 1857 led to Napoleon's decision to intervene. Demanding that all attacks against missionaries be halted, he sent a naval force to Vietnam which captured Saigon in 1859. A treaty, signed three years later, granted France control of the city and its three surrounding provinces. The French, hoping that the Mekong might serve as a trade route into the interior of China, soon extended their control, and by 1874 all of southern Vietnam was under their authority.

In 1880 the emperor of Vietnam, **Tu-Doc,** tried to fight back. As a measure of his desperation, he appealed to his nation's age-old enemy—China—for help. He died three years later, just after the French, having turned their attention north, had taken Hanoi. Strife between rival factions in the imperial court had made it difficult to organize resistance to the French, and on June 6, 1884, at Hué, Vietnam signed a treaty agreeing to recognize French control. French troops battled briefly with a Chinese army in northern Vietnam, but in 1885 China agreed to French control of Vietnam. By 1893 France had extended its holdings over what are now the countries of Laos and Cambodia and appeared to be in firm control of all of Indochina for good.

SECTION 1 REVIEW

1. **Vocabulary to Know** Mekong Delta, central highlands, northern highlands, Red River Delta, coastal lowlands, Nam-Viet, Dai Viet

2. **People to Identify** Gia-Long, Pigneau de Béhaine, Minh Mang, Napoleon III, Tu-Doc

3. What are the five main land regions of Vietnam?

4. For what reasons did China become interested in Vietnam? What was the result?

5. When did the Vietnamese free themselves of Chinese rule?

6. When did France first seize Vietnamese territory? Why were the French interested in Vietnam?

7. **Critical Thinking** What might the Vietnamese emperors have done to be in a better position to resist the French?

2 FRENCH COLONIAL RULE LEAVES ITS MARK ON VIETNAM

Vietnam, which possessed a strong sense of nationhood and civilization, was firmly and unhappily under French control by the late 1800's. In an effort to destroy national unity, the French divided Vietnam into three parts: the southern third of the country was known as **Cochinchina,** the center was called **Annam,** and the north was **Tonkin.** Their rule of Vietnam showed the worst face of **imperialism**—the takeover of another country to gain economic and policial advantages.

   French Colonial Policy In its rule of overseas colonies, France followed a policy of **assimilation.** Under this policy, people were expected to absorb the ideas and culture of the home country. Believing that they had achieved the highest level of civilization in the world, the French regarded their colonial subjects as children, to be brought up in the exact image of their French "parents."
   To back up their ideals of assimilation, the French in Indochina depended on force to keep their administration in place. It took 5,000 French officials to govern a population of 30 million

people—the same number of British officials who were managing India, which had more than ten times as many inhabitants.

Although a handful of Vietnamese were favored and brought into the administration—many of them Catholics who had learned a smattering of French from the missionaries—they were given little responsibility and low salaries. The lowliest French official always earned more in the colonial system than the highest-ranking Vietnamese.

In the villages, meanwhile, the French relied on local leaders for such tasks as collecting taxes and raising labor forces for public projects. These village leaders almost always used their power to oppress the peasants and embezzle funds. The villagers' misery, then, was forced on them by their fellow Vietnamese. Although French responsibility for this was recognized, the seeds for a social revolution as well as a struggle for independence were being planted.

French Justice As part of their rule in Indochina, the French introduced their own system of justice. Guided by good intentions, French judges were shocked by such traditional Vietnamese practices as the beheading of thieves or the trampling by elephants of adultrous women. The French judicial system, however, created strains in Vietnamese society. No longer did the father resolve family squabbles. Neither could a respected elder be called in to mediate a village dispute. Finally, a system which preached equal justice but in which political suspects were jailed for years without trial was one which never gained credibility.

Economic Policies Remembering his days as governor-general of Indochina, **Paul Doumer** wrote in his memoirs, "When France arrived in Indochina, the Annamites were ripe for servitude." It was Doumer who transformed Indochina from a financial drain for France to a profitable enterprise. In so doing, his economic policies had a profound impact on traditional society.

In its conquest of Vietnam, France had spent great sums of money. Even worse, Cochinchina, Annam, and Tonkin were running budget deficits, mostly from lack of organization. When Doumer arrived in Vietnam in 1897, his first priority was to centralize authority. After imposing his will on Vietnam—especially on the French bankers, merchants, and landowners who were running Cochinchina as their own separate colony—Doumer set about funneling customs duties and direct taxes into his central treasury. He then came up with the idea of creating official monopolies to produce and sell salt, alcohol, and opium.

Imported opium had been smoked in small quantities before the arrival of the French, though only by Vietnam's Chinese residents. But when Doumer built a refinery in Saigon, opium consumption was encouraged. Revenues from the sale of opium rose so fast that they later accounted for one third of the colonial administration's income. The money flowing into the colonial coffers meant, however, that there were growing numbers of drug addicts. Decades later, the effect of Doumer's decision would be felt by the American military.

Greater than the impact to Vietnamese society brought by the opium monopoly, was Doumer's land policy. Before the French arrival, most Vietnamese peasants had owned land. To spur rice exports, however, Doumer encouraged land-grabbing by prominent Vietnamese and French families.

By the 1930's, as much as 70 percent of Vietnam's peasants were landless tenants. Most of them worked as tenant farmers. Under the terms of their service, they owed a landlord 40 to 50 percent of their harvests as rent. (Even 70 percent of their harvests was not unusual.) When they suffered poor harvests, they had no choice but to borrow money from the landlord. They were then forced to work until the debt was repaid, a virtual impossibility. They thus became debt slaves to their landlords.

Under the French, Vietnam became one of the world's largest exporters of rice. And the large number of landless peasants that had been created suited another purpose: cheap labor was available for work on rubber plantations, coal mines, and construction projects. Between 1916 and 1930, the land under rubber cultivation increased five times to 250,000 acres. Ten years later, just six companies—all entirely French-held—owned 90 percent of the plantations. Working in appalling conditions on the planations, one of every twenty rubber workers died of malaria.

Working conditions were equally bad in the coal mines. The coal industry was even more concentrated than rubber; two companies produced over 90 percent of the total output. The vast Hongay coal mines in Tonkin, in the words of an American journalist in 1927, owned "everything from the bowels of the earth to the slightest sprig of grass that may force its way through the coal dust."

By the time Doumer left Indochina—he was later elected President of France—the colony was in the black. He had tied Vietnam to the French economic system as a provider of raw materials and as a market for France's merchandise. (In spite of all the rubber that Vietnam exported, for instance, virtually every finished rubber product had to be imported from France.) In so doing, French taxpayers had been relieved of any financial burden. There were, then, few anticolonial voices at home, while French business interests were free to exploit Indochina at will.

The Growth of Nationalism In Vietnam, however, there was smoldering resentment to French rule. Guerrilla activity would flare up from time to time, only to be brutally crushed. Meanwhile, leaders in the movement to oust the French were rising to prominence. Many were exceptional young Vietnamese—usually from wealthy families—who had been able to travel overseas or study in Paris. After years abroad, where they enjoyed comparative freedom, their return home was painful. They rarely found good jobs, and their pay was always less than that of the lowest French officials, who treated them like servants. Many such returned Vietnamese became **nationalists,** supporters of independence.

Ho Chi Minh The leading nationalist to emerge during the colonial era was **Ho Chi Minh.** Originally named Nguyen Sinh Cung, Ho was born in 1890 in a village of Nghe An province in central Vietnam. His father, an official at the imperial court of Hué, quit his job, abandoning his wife and children to roam the countryside as a wandering teacher.

Like his father, Ho soon began a wandering life of his own. As a young man, he left Vietnam in 1911 to work aboard a French liner. Thirty years passed before he returned to Vietnam.

Ho spent nearly three years at sea, stopping at ports around the world. On one voyage he arrived in New York City, where he disembarked and settled as an itinerant laborer. The fact that Chinese immigrants to America enjoyed the legal rights of citizens impressed him greatly.

After a year in the United States, Ho sailed to London where he found work in a hotel. Toward the end of World War I he went to France, which at the time was teeming with Vietnamese soldiers fighting on the Allied side. New ideas were in the air as well. In Paris he joined the circle around Phan Chu Trinh, an early opponent of French rule, and quickly emerged as a leader of Vietnamese nationalists living in France.

The Versailles Conference In the meantime, President Woodrow Wilson arrived in Paris in 1919 for the **Versailles Conference,** which formally ended World War I. Ho drafted a statement to hand the American President, writing that "all subject peoples are filled with hopes by the prospect that an era of right and justice is opening to them." His appeal asked for constitutional government and other reforms in Vietnam—but not outright independence.

Ho failed to meet with Wilson, and the peace conference quickly dismissed his petition. But he had attracted the attention of leading French Socialists who invited him to attend their congress in December, 1920, at the town of Tours. At that meeting, Ho joined with a group of breakaway party members to form the French Communist Party. Claiming years later that "it was patriotism and not communism that originally inspired me," he believed that only a Soviet-inspired, world-wide revolution would free Vietnam from French rule.

Ho left France for the Soviet Union in 1924 to study revolutionary methods. Now in his own words a "professional revolutionary," he traveled to China where, among other things, he began to mobilize Vietnamese students in the Revolutionary Youth League.

The Indochinese Communist Party Through the 1920's, the revolutionary climate in Vietnam remained bleak, with sporadic uprisings quickly put down. During one revolt in Ho's native Nghe An province, peasants temporarily set up their own government, leading Ho to believe mistakenly that a revolutionary opportunity had arrived. Uniting three rival factions, he founded the **Indochinese Communist Party** at a secret meeting in Hong Kong in June, 1929. Having long since abandoned his moderate requests of Woodrow Wilson from ten years before, Ho now called for Vietnamese independence and a revolutionary government.

SECTION 2 REVIEW

1. **Vocabulary to Know** Cochinchina, Annam, Tonkin, imperialism, assimilation, nationalist, Versailles Conference, Indochinese Communist Party

2. **People to Identify** Paul Doumer, Ho Chi Minh

3. How did French administrators regard their colonial subjects?

4. Why did the French introduce their own system of justice? What effect did it have?

5. What evidence is there of Ho's revolutionary commitment?

6. **Critical Thinking** Why did the French land policy have the greatest impact on Vietnamese society?

3 THE JAPANESE OCCUPATION LEADS TO INDEPENDENCE

In the spring of 1940, world events swept over Southeast Asia. World War II had broken out the year before in Europe, and now Japanese forces began pouring down from China, taking over French Indochina. Soon they would occupy the Philippines, Indonesia, and Malaya. Nationalists throughout Southeast Asia welcomed the Japanese, and in many cases cooperated actively with them. Ho Chi Minh, however, opposed the replacement of one colonial master by another. Aligning himself with the Allies, he looked forward to the defeat of Japan. In return, he expected to win independence for his country.

The Vietminh Early in 1941 Ho, disguised as a Chinese journalist, slipped back into Vietnam for the first time in thirty years. Quickly he formed a new organization, led by Communists, to be made up of "patriots of all ages and all types, peasants, workers, merchants, and soldiers." The movement was called the Vietnam Independence League—better known as the **Vietminh.** Ho, who for protection and disguise had used countless names in his overseas travels, borrowed from the movement what was to become his official pseudonym, Ho Chi Minh—"Bringer of Light."

Japanese Occupation The goal of the Vietminh was not only to fight the Japanese occupiers but the French as well. In what today might seem an ironic, or certainly unusual, circumstance the Japanese allowed the French administration in Indochina to remain in place. Actually, the Japanese were only following the example of the Germans in Europe who, after occupying northern France in 1940, at first allowed Marshal Pétain to maintain a puppet regime in the southern portion of the country. (A **puppet** is someone who appears to be in authority while being controlled by someone else.) Similarly, the Japanese, who originally intended to use Vietnam only as a springboard to the rest of Asia, were content to direct the French from behind the scenes. The French, who wanted to keep their colony, had no choice but to **collaborate** (that is, cooperate) with the victorious Japanese.

As the occupation went on, the Japanese inevitably began to meddle in Vietnamese affairs. They were happy to support a religious sect called **Cao Dai,** which had gained great strength in Cochinchina in the years since its founding in 1919. The cult, whose "saints" included Jesus, Buddha, Victor Hugo, Sun Yat-sen, and Joan of Arc, organized its own private army with Japanese backing. The Japanese also encouraged the **Hoa Hao,** a Buddhist sect that was attracting the support of thousands of peasants.

Vo Nguyen Giap The Vietminh, meanwhile, had got off to a rough start, in large part because of the absence of their leader, Ho Chi Minh. Late in 1941, Ho crossed into China hoping to seek help from anti-Japanese forces operating there. No sooner had he left Vietnam than a local warlord slammed him into prison, where he remained for more than a year.

Inside Vietnam, the Vietminh slowly began to take shape under **Vo Nguyen Giap**, a figure who would occupy his nation's center stage for years to come. Giap had been educated in colonial Vietnam's finest schools, earning a law degree from the University of Hanoi. One day in 1941 his young wife—sentenced to a French prison for nationalist activities—died along with his infant child. From then on, he never lost his hatred of colonialism.

American Help During the war years, the U.S. Office of Strategic Services (OSS) supplied the Vietminh with some small arms and ammunition. The Vietminh, in return, rescued downed American pilots and provided the United States with information about the movement of Japanese forces. The help from the OSS led Ho to expect that the United States would back Vietnam's demand for independence.

With the Vietminh eager for a small victory that would gain them local support, Giap overwhelmed two remote French posts on Christmas Eve, 1944, capturing arms and ammunition. Soon he was attacking larger bases, and the Vietminh's gold-starred red flag was flying over villages throughout northern Vietnam.

The Japanese Surrender By the end of 1944, as American forces under the command of General **Douglas MacArthur** were reconquering the Philippines, it was obvious that the days of the Japanese were numbered. **Charles De Gaulle,** head of the government that was now in power in newly liberated France, feared the Americans might head toward Indochina and link up with the Vietnamese nationalists. Determined that Indochina should be restored to French rule, De Gaulle began sending agents and arms into the region.

Within months, however, news of Japan's surrender reached Vietnam, and now the countryside was convulsed with peasant uprisings. In part the uprisings were the direct result of a devastating famine, caused by the Japanese who, in the last years of the war,

THE HISTORY OF VIETNAM TO 1954

had forced peasant farmers to plant such industrial crops as jute and peanuts instead of rice. Two million of the ten million people in northern Vietnam starved to death. Amidst the turmoil, and with the power vacuum created by the defeat of Japan, Ho Chi Minh recognized that the time had come to seize power.

Independence Declared On August 16, 1945, Ho formed a National Liberation Committee and named himself as president. Vietminh units entered Hanoi on that same day, seizing public buildings as Japanese troops stood by. A week later, carried on a stretcher from his jungle headquarters, a sickly Ho arrived in the city. He set to work on a portable typewriter, drafting Vietnam's declaration of independence.

On September 2, 1945, speaking through a simple microphone to a crowd in Ba Dinh Square, Ho opened with the words, "We hold the truth that all men are created equal, that they are endowed by their Creator with certain unalienable rights, among them life, liberty, and the pursuit of happiness." Later in the day, during the independence celebrations, American warplanes flew over head, United States Army officers joined Vo Nguyen Giap on the reviewing stand, and a Vietnamese band played the "Star-Spangled Banner."

Few people in Hanoi would have recognized the passage from the American Declaration of Independence or been familiar with the American national anthem. But Ho, a deeply committed Communist, was practical enough to allow the United States to play a prominent role at the birth of modern Vietnam for a very good reason. Casting about for international support for Vietnamese independence, he feared that it would be only a matter of weeks before the French returned in force. He was right.

SECTION 3 REVIEW

1. **Vocabulary to Know** Vietminh, puppet, collaborate, Cao Dai, Hoa Hao

2. **People to Identify** Vo Nguyen Giap, Douglas MacArthur, Charles De Gaulle

3. What was Ho Chi Minh's position regarding the Japanese occupation?

4. What role did the French play during the Japanese occupation?

5. What side did the United States favor during the war years? Why?

6. **Critical Thinking** What leadership qualities did Ho Chi Minh demonstrate during the Vietnamese independence celebrations?

4 THE WAR WITH FRANCE BEGINS

At the time of Ho's declaration of independence, Vietnam was in chaos. Rival Vietnamese were fighting each other or clashing with the French. Meanwhile, at the **Potsdam Conference,** held by the Allies near the end of World War II to plan the future, a scheme had been devised to disarm the Japanese in Vietnam. The Chinese Nationalists, the delegates at Potsdam agreed, would occupy the north while the British would move into the south.

The French Return The French merchants and officials still in Vietnam were unhappy with the Potsdam decision. So was the French government. Events soon led to intervention by the French army.

Following a rampage by unruly French paratroopers and Foreign Legionnaires through Vietnamese neighborhoods in Saigon, Vietminh leaders called a general strike on September 24, 1945. Because of the conflict that started immediately thereafter, that date is often regarded as the beginning of the first Indochinese war.

Saigon's 20,000 French civilians, fearing the worst as the strike began, barricaded their houses. Vietminh squads attacked locations throughout the city, and, in one brutal episode, massacred 150 French civilians in a residential suburb. Other hostages were dragged away and mutilated.

The British, with their home economy devastated by six years of war, had few troops in the area. To restore order, they decided on a temporary, yet incredible measure—to rearm the Japanese. General of the Army Douglas MacArthur, following events from his command in Tokyo, was indignant:

> If there is anything that makes my blood boil, it is to see our allies in Indochina . . . deploying Japanese troops to reconquer the . . . people we promised to liberate. It is the most ignoble kind of betrayal.

Soon the British decided to transport French forces back into the region. Dashing Ho's hopes, the United States agreed to the plan.

THE HISTORY OF VIETNAM TO 1954

Commanded by **Jacques Philippe Leclerc**, whose forces had helped liberate Paris the year before, the French arrived in October. By early 1946, Leclerc announced confidently that the Vietminh had been crushed. At the same time, under the terms of the Potsdam Conference 180,000 Chinese Nationalists had arrived in the north.

Confronted with the Chinese presence, Ho Chi Minh concluded that he had no choice but to ask the French back—on condition that they honor Vietnam's independence. Under a compromise reached on March 6, 1946, France recognized Vietnam as a free state within the French Union in return for being allowed to keep 25,000 troops in the country. The French also agreed to hold an election in Cochinchina to determine whether it should be joined with the rest of Vietnam. The referendum was never held, and the French governor of the region soon established a government, firmly controlled by France, in Saigon.

Unhappy with the agreement he had reached with the French, Ho had at least found a way to rid Vietnam of the Chinese. As he told critics of the plan:

> You fools! Don't you realize what it means if the Chinese remain? Don't you remember your history? The last time the Chinese came, they stayed 1,000 years. The French are foreigners. They are weak. Colonialism is dying. The white man is finished in Asia. But if the Chinese stay now, they will never go.

Fighting in the North Despite the agreement with the French, it was clear from the start that peace would not last. French public opinion, for one thing, opposed any kind of compromise. Every political party—from the most conservative to the Communists—longed to restore the national prestige that France had lost to Germany in 1940. Restoring the colonies to their prewar status seemed one way to do it.

The short-lived agreement between France and the Vietminh came apart at the port city of Haiphong. After a minor dispute in November, 1946, with Vietminh representatives over the right to collect customs duties, French armored units attacked the city. Airplanes dropped bombs, while ships anchored in the harbor lobbed shells into the city. It was soon over, with entire neighborhoods destroyed and at least 6,000 Vietnamese civilians killed.

Within a month fighting had broken out in Hanoi, France's former capital of all Indochina. Poorly equipped, with arms ranging from ancient muskets to spears and swords, the Vietminh fought street to street against French machine guns, heavy artillery, and tanks. Fighting raged through December, with the French finally taking control.

During the battle for Hanoi, Ho appealed to the United States and Great Britain to restrain the French. The West had grown increasingly suspicious of Ho, however. As a Communist, he was seen in many quarters as part of the Soviet Union's plan for worldwide domination. France's efforts to hold on to Vietnam had become part of a larger international contest, one which involved the United States.

Containment and American Aid By the end of World War II, tensions had begun to appear in the relations between the Western powers and the Soviet Union. These tensions would soon grow into a bitter rivalry known as the **cold war.** Early in 1946, George Kennan, a leading State Department expert on Russia, pointed out that in the future the United States would have to resist Soviet expansion, wherever it occurred. Many Western leaders agreed with Kennan and his policy, which became known as **containment.** They compared the threat to that of Hitler's Germany which, they believed, should have been aggressively challenged in the 1930's. Soon, as the Soviets strengthened their domination of Eastern Europe, containment become a cornerstone of American foreign policy.

In the first years after peace was restored in Europe, there was real concern of a Communist electoral victory in France itself. Economic stagnation and political instability were sapping the country's strength, and moderate French politicians warned that American interference in colonial matters would play into the hands of the powerful French Communist Party. As a result, the United States decided to let France handle Vietnam in its own way.

Other events convinced the United States that it was following the correct policy. One was the takeover in 1949 of China by the Communist forces of **Mao Zedong.** President **Harry S. Truman** quickly asserted that the containment policy, at first focused on Europe, would be extended to Asia. The second event was the invasion of South Korea by Communist North Korea in June, 1950. Finally, having given up on reaching an agreement with the West, Ho Chi Minh persuaded Communist China and the Soviet Union to recognize his Democratic Republic of Vietnam. Secretary of State **Dean Acheson** reflected the Truman administration's view when he held that Soviet recognition "should remove any illusions as to the 'nationalist' nature of Ho Chi Minh's aims, and reveals Ho in his true colors as the mortal enemy of native independence in Indochina."

It was Acheson who, late in 1949, persuaded Truman to earmark $15 million in aid to the French forces in Indochina. Congress approved the appropriation in 1950, the first of the more than $2 billion that would be sent to the French over the next four years. Indeed, American aid became so crucial that by 1954 the United States was paying 80 percent of France's military costs in Indochina.

The United States also recognized the government of **Bao Dai,** who had been set up as a puppet emperor in 1949. Several State Department officials objected to this move. In the words of one expert, Raymond B. Fosdick, "Whether the French like it or not, independence is coming to Indochina. Why, therefore, do we tie ourselves to the tail of their battered kite?" For most administation figures, however, the French effort in Vietnam had become a stand against Soviet expansion.

The War Drags On In the early days of the conflict, it appeared to many observers that the French would easily defeat the Vietminh. The French forces far outnumbered those of the Vietminh, and were able to gain control of the major cities and highways. Officials predicted, in fact, that the war would be over in three months, not quite soon enough to get the boys home for Christmas.

The Vietminh, meanwhile, learned much from the success of Mao Zedong in China. Giap and other Vietminh military leaders studied Mao's teachings carefully. One of the most important lessons was that no military unit should confront the enemy unless the enemy were outnumbered. The result was that the Vietminh rarely fought any pitched battles. Instead, small bands of guerrillas lay in ambush along roads and trails, attacking the advancing enemy before disappearing into the jungle. They also moved at night, cutting off enemy supply and communications lines, and disappearing before dawn.

Ho Chi Minh, meeting in 1947 with American journalist David Schoenbrun, described the Vietminh as guerrilla "tigers" who would eventually defeat the French colonial "elephant":

> It will be a war between an elephant and a tiger. If the tiger ever stands still, the elephant will crush him with his mighty tusks. But the tiger will not stand still.... He will leap upon the back of the elephant, tearing huge chunks from his side, and then he will leap back into the dark jungle. And slowly the elephant will bleed to death. That will be the war in Indochina.

And so the war dragged on, with the French unable to lure the Vietminh into a major battle where they could be decisively defeated and with the Vietminh unable to drive the French from the country. From the start, however, Ho knew that time was on his side. "You can kill ten of my men for every one I kill of yours," he told a French visitor. "But even at those odds, you will lose and I will win."

Support from China In 1949 the Vietminh received a big boost with the defeat in China of Chiang Kai-shek's Nationalists. At once the victorious Communists began supplying the Vietminh with important military aid, including automatic weapons, mortars, howitzers, and even trucks. Thousands of men and women, enduring months of backbreaking travel on foot, transported the Chinese supplies. In addition, Ho's forces could operate safely out of bases behind the Chinese border. Soon, the Vietminh was no longer a ragtag collection of guerrillas, but a real army.

La Sale Guerre By the end of 1952, the Vietminh were wearing down the French, and there was little enthusiasm at home for what was now called *la sale guerre*—the dirty little war. With more than 90,000 French dead, wounded, or missing in action, and with the appropriation of large sums of money, the war was costing the nation dearly.

On the battlefield too, frustration was growing. The French did their best to adapt to guerrilla warfare. Describing one specially formed commando unit, a Frenchman recalled, "They were lions! Nothing they couldn't do. Their specialty was to attack naked, but well greased all over, with their ammo slung round their bellies." One night, he continued, when the troops were lined up and ready for combat, the commanding officer "was in the raw, everybody was. He saw the chaplain in line, and was *shocked*. 'Father, not you!' he said. 'At least put your shirt on!'"

In spite of these heroics, the French continued to face the same problem: the Vietminh would flee in the face of superior force. In the words of one French colonel, "We always had the feeling we were plunging a knife into water." With the new year, however, came a new commander in chief, General **Henri Navarre,** who believed he knew how to end the stalemated war.

A New French Strategy General Navarre, a career officer who had fought in two world wars, was supremely confident in his abilities. Highly optimistic, he forecast success, saying, in words that would be echoed often in the decade to come, "Now we can see it clearly—like light at the end of a tunnel."

THE HISTORY OF VIETNAM TO 1954

Navarre's plan was to assign friendly Vietnamese troops the task of defending the southern part of the country against the Vietminh. Then, a major part of the French army would move into northern Vietnam near Laos, creating an inviting target for the enemy to attack in force. When that happened, Navarre believed, the superior French troops would defeat the Vietminh and take control of the north.

In planning his strategy, Navarre made several major errors. First, he underestimated the strength of the force opposing him, thinking still of the Vietminh as scattered guerrilla bands. He even refused to believe intelligence sources that accurately described the Vietminh strength.

Navarre's second error was to reject the idea that the Vietminh could move enough military arms and supplies through the jungles and hills of northern Vietnam to back up an attack on a fortified camp. Third, he underestimated the Vietminh's tactics, assuming they would recklessly unleash a "human wave" assault against his fortified positions.

The Battle of Dienbienphu Begins The place that Navarre chose for his showdown with Giap's forces was the remote village of **Dienbienphu,** located in a broad valley surrounded by jungle-covered hills in the northwestern corner of Vietnam. Twelve battalions of French troops were dispatched to Dienbienphu late in 1953. By the time they had fortified the area and built an airstrip, they numbered 13,000 (with about half qualified for combat). Surrounding them were some 50,000 Vietminh, with another 20,000 strung out along supply lines. Somehow the Vietminh had managed to move heavy artillery guns along camouflaged jungle trails and had positioned them in the hills overlooking the French positions.

When the Vietminh attack began, it was in fact a "human wave" assault, just as Navarre had predicted. But after taking heavy losses, Giap called off the attack and completely changed his strategy. He issued an order to "strangle" the French by encircling them with tunnels and trenches. He also knew that the French were eager for a battle and that a long delay would destroy their morale. He knew too that by waiting another month or two, rain and fog would descend on the valley. This would prevent the French from flying in supplies and fresh troops, and would keep French planes from attacking Vietminh positions.

The attack was delayed until the evening of March 13, 1954, when suddenly every heavy gun in the Vietminh arsenal opened fire on the French garrison. Telephone lines were cut, the airstrip was pocked with shell holes, and many French guns—foolishly left unprotected—were put out of action. Within 24 hours, the Vietminh had seized two hills overlooking the fortress in the valley below. Quickly, their heavy guns knocked out the airport, making resupply impossible except by parachute drop.

Over the next days, Giap began closing in on Dienbienphu. His forces would emerge from specially built tunnels, dug right up to the edge of the French bunkers, to engage in hand-to-hand combat. Slowly, one outpost in the valley after another was overrun, and the noose around Dienbienphu grew tighter. The French quickly realized that unless they received outside help—and fast—that they would be doomed.

VIETNAM FACT

The French army that served in Indochina was not really French. The 150,000-man force was a classic colonial army. Along with French volunteers, soldiers came from Morocco, Senegal, Cambodia, Vietnam—from all the French colonies. (No French draftees were ever sent to Indochina.) In addition, there was the French Foreign Legion. This famed force of professional mercenaries was made up largely of foreigners who were led by French officers. Germans formed the largest contingent in the Legion, and German was jokingly said to be the war's second language. At the war's end, when the figures for the dead and wounded were counted, a majority of the French casualties were found not to be French.

An Appeal to the United States French reinforcements bravely parachuted into the beleaguered camp. Many were killed or wounded by Vietminh fire before they hit the ground. Clearly, outside help was needed to turn the tide.

Given the emergency, General **Paul Ely,** chief of staff of the French army, flew from Paris to Washington, D.C., to plead for help. He met there with top-ranking officials, including President **Dwight D. Eisenhower.** His request: that American bombers launch massive air strikes against the Communist forces closing in on Dienbienphu. Unless the United States moved quickly, he argued, France would be driven from Indochina.

The Americans treated Ely's request seriously. They had, after all, invested significant sums of money in France's military efforts. And at a press conference in early April, 1954, President

THE HISTORY OF VIETNAM TO 1954

Eisenhower told the American people, "The loss of Indochina will cause the fall of Southeast Asia like a set of dominos." (This view would soon become known as the **domino theory**.)

Many top officials were in favor of entering the war. Some, including Vice President Richard Nixon, tried to get Congress to authorize the President to employ air power, but several influential senators and representatives—Senator Lyndon Johnson among them—turned down the request. There was even talk of ending the siege quickly through the use of atomic weapons or of airlifting American ground troops to fight alongside the French.

In the end, Eisenhower agreed with Army Chief of Staff **Matthew Ridgway** that getting bogged down in a major war in Asia would be a mistake, particularly without the participation of other allies (and no such participation was likely). Elected on a peace platform and having recently overseen a truce agreement signed to end the Korean conflict, moreover, Eisenhower turned down the French request.

The Fall of Dienbienphu All the time the Eisenhower administration was debating France's plea for help, the Vietminh were tightening their grip around Dienbienphu. Foot by foot they advanced as the French supply of food and ammunition dwindled. Eventually the French defenses, once about fifteen miles around, had shrunk to the size of Yankee Stadium. With orders to defend their positions to the death, the French soldiers fought desperately. One legionnaire told how he brought a wounded soldier back to a camp hospital:

> He had a piece of lead as big as my fist in his thigh.... I found him the next morning. He'd slapped on a rough dressing then gone off to rejoin his section in an attack. His body was riddled with bullets.

Finally, on May 7, 1954, the Vietminh overran the camp's final few hundred yards. A French soldier recalled the horror of the last attack. "A shell burst right in our trench," he remembered, "and the legionnaire next to me disintegrated.... Death was spitting all round, and men falling like flies."

During the 55-day battle, French casualties numbered 3,000 dead, more than 5,000 wounded, and about 11,000 captured. During their 500-mile march to Vietminh prison camps, thousands of the captured troops died of exhaustion and exposure. The Vietminh casualties were even higher—about 8,000 killed and 15,000 wounded. But to Ho Chi Minh the sacrifice was worthwhile. France's seven-and-a-half-year effort to regain its empire in Indochina had been ended. By coincidence, on the day after the red flag of the Vietminh went up over the French command bunker at Dienbienphu, nine delegations assembled in Geneva, Switzerland. The item on their agenda was to decide the future of Indochina.

SECTION 4 REVIEW

1. **Vocabulary to Know** Potsdam Conference, cold war, containment, Dienbienphu, domino theory

2. **People to Identify** Jacques Philippe Leclerc, Harry S. Truman, Dean Acheson, Bao Dai, Henri Navarre, Paul Ely, Dwight D. Eisenhower, Matthew Ridgway

3. Why did the French return to southern Vietnam? To northern Vietnam?

4. How did the cold war affect American policy in Vietnam?

5. What mistakes did the French generals make at Dienbienphu?

6. **Critical Thinking** Why can the Battle of Dienbienphu be considered a turning point in the history of Southeast Asia?

5 THE GENEVA PEACE CONFERENCE DIVIDES VIETNAM

The aim of the **Geneva Conference,** which opened in late April, 1954, was to find permanent peace settlements for both Korea and Vietnam. Attending the meeting were all of the governments involved in the wars in Southeast Asia.

No settlement was found to the Korean situation. The truce there continued, as it does today, with the country divided. As for Vietnam, the conference delegates did even worse, creating new problems.

The Conference Begins The participants at Geneva met with an unusual timetable spurring them on. After the talks had at first seemed to be going nowhere, a French deputy rose in the Chamber of Deputies (France's parliament) and asked for that body's endorsement as France's new premier. **Pierre Mendès-France** then electrified France with this plea: "I promise to resign," he said,

THE HISTORY OF VIETNAM TO 1954

"if, one month from now, on July 20, I have failed to obtain a cease-fire in Indochina." If there were no peace in a month, he went on to say, his last act as head of France's government would be to send draftees to Indochina. To make clear that he was serious, Mendès-France ordered large numbers of French conscripts to be innoculated for yellow fever.

The day after Mendès-France's speech, the Chamber overwhelmingly endorsed him. Acting as his own foreign minister, he immediately headed for Geneva.

The mood in Geneva was one of deep mistrust. The heads of the French and Vietminh delegations were not speaking to one another. **John Foster Dulles,** the American Secretary of State, had already left the conference. In the short time he was in attendance he had made waves by refusing even to shake the hand of China's delegate, **Zhou Enlai.** (Dulles growled that they might meet again only in the event of their cars colliding.) The Vietminh avoided Emperor Bao Dai's representative while mistrusting the motives of the Chinese.

The Role of China With the arrival of Mendès-France, Zhou Enlai saw a chance to break the deadlock. He took charge of the talks for the Communist side and entered into long, secret sessions with the French newcomer.

France, of course, had obvious reasons for seeking a cease-fire. Already the Vietminh controlled three quarters of Vietnam, and now they were making new gains. China had its own reasons for desiring a speedy settlement. For one thing, the Chinese wanted to make a good impression in this, their debut in international diplomacy. More importantly, they had just suffered a million casualties in Korea, a conflict that had nearly spilled over into Chinese territory. Zhou now sought to avoid another land war in Asia, one that might again involve the United States.

China's goal, then, was a settlement allowing the French to stay in Vietnam while keeping the Americans out. The best way to reach this goal, Zhou quickly saw, was to divide Vietnam into two zones—one Communist-controlled and one backed by France. This was, of course, a direct blow to Ho Chi Minh's dream of a united country. But as one of Zhou's deputies explained to a French delegate, "We are here to re-establish peace, not to back the Vietminh."

Partition Mendès-France came around to the idea of **partition,** or division. Where, though, should the dividing line be drawn? The Vietminh, under pressure from the Soviets and Chinese, agreed to the **principle** of partition but only if the line were drawn at the thirteenth parallel (giving them two thirds of the country). Mendès-France suggested the eighteenth parallel.

As the haggling continued, and as Mendès-France's deadline approached, the Soviet delegate, Vyacheslav Molotov, announced, "Let's agree on the seventeenth." And so the **seventeenth parallel** was chosen, dividing Vietnam roughly in half.

A Call for Elections Partition was seen by the Geneva participants as a temporary measure designed to halt the fighting by separating the two sides. Elections to unify Vietnam would follow. Now the delegates debated when those elections should be held. The Vietminh, eager to take advantage of their battlefield strength, wanted elections within six months. That was too soon for the French. Again, it was Molotov who made the decision. "Shall we say two years?" he offered.

An Assessment of Geneva As the delegates signed the cease-fire accords ending the fighting in Indochina, it was painfully clear that the Geneva agreement had postponed a settlement rather than reach one. It should be noted that the agreement between France and the Vietminh on elections was an oral agreement only. As both sides began withdrawing their forces north or south of the partition line, the election question would loom large in the future.

Mendès-France, in meeting his timetable, ironically had achieved more for France at the conference table than the generals had won on the battlefield. The Vietminh, on the other hand, left Geneva disappointed and muttering about being double-crossed by the Chinese.

"The Blessed Virgin Is Moving South" As part of the Geneva Accords there was to be a 300-day period during which people could move north or south of the seventeenth parallel. Some 120,000 Vietminh militants moved north. But it was the avalanche of people heading south that made world headlines.

The French, offering transportation to any Vietnamese wishing to leave, had estimated that no more than 30,000 people would depart. Instead, nearly a million refugees, most of them penniless, clamored to take up the offer. American, British, and Nationalist Chinese boats and planes were rushed to the scene to handle this enormous movement of people.

Among the Vietnamese who left were those who had served in the French colonial government. They were joined by people who had favored the nationalist cause but had refused to back the Vietminh. The great majority, however, were Catholics. An estimated 60 percent of North Vietnam's 1.5 million Catholics joined the refugees.

American propaganda may have played a part in the decision of many Catholics to leave, for the United States understood that the northerners would provide the government in southern Vietnam with strong anti-Communist support. The U.S. Information Agency distributed posters showing Communist henchmen closing churches and forcing people to pray under a picture of Ho Chi Minh. Slogans such as "The Blessed Virgin Is Moving South" were also used in American propaganda. But propaganda cannot completely account for the mass flight. As one observer explained, "People just don't pull up their roots and transplant themselves because of slogans. They honestly feared what might happen to them, and the emotion was strong enough to overcome their attachment to their land, their homes, and their ancestral graves."

Problems in the North The flight of the Catholics had an advantage for Ho Chi Minh because it quickly removed potential opponents from his territory. Returning to Hanoi in October, 1954, for the first time in eight years, he had to deal with other problems facing his regime.

Most of the fighting against the French had taken place in the north, and the country was devastated. Buildings were destroyed, bridges blown up, factories stripped of tools and machinery. Most critically, with the loss of the south, a traditional source of rice had been removed. Only massive rice imports in 1955, financed by the Soviet Union, prevented a new famine.

Ho and Land Reform The need to import rice provided Ho with an opportunity to address the question of land reform. Motivated by ideology, he saw a means of reaching one of his cherished goals—the **collectivization** of farming. (To collectivize is to bring together, under state control, the livestock, equipment, and buildings of many small farmers on to one large tract of land.)

To achieve his goal, Ho turned against peasants branded by his regime as "landlords." In actuality very few peasants in the North farmed more than three of four acres. Nevertheless, Communist leaders concluded that "landlords," representing 2 percent of the population, would have to be done away with. Villages were given **quotas,** or assigned numbers, and were ordered to begin rounding up suspects.

As many as 10,000 people were killed in the land reform, while perhaps 100,000 others were made to work in forced labor camps. Finally, in 1956, Ho halted the program and publicly confessed that "errors have been committed." Thousands of survivors were released from the camps, but tension continued. In Ho's native Nghe An province, scene of an uprising against the French 26 years earlier (page 10), peasants again defied the government. After soldiers broke up a group of peasants who were presenting a petition to Canadian commissioners monitoring the armistice, violence broke out. Responding in the same manner as the French, Ho sent a division of troops to put down the rebellion. Some 6,000 peasants were killed or deported in the campaign.

In the end, the Communist leadership was pleased with its campaign to collectivize farming. More and more poor peasants were forced onto state-run farms, accounting by the end of the decade for almost 60 percent of all farming families.

As Ho brutally strengthened power in the North, a new government was being formed south of the seventeenth parallel. That government would, in a short time, replace the French with American backers. American involvement in Vietnam would grow.

SECTION 5 REVIEW

1. **Vocabulary to Know** Geneva Conference, partition, seventeenth parallel, collectivization, quota

2. **People to Identify** Pierre Mendès-France, John Foster Dulles, Zhou Enlai

3. What promise did Pierre Mendès-France make to the people of France?

4. Why was China eager to help solve the Vietnam conflict?

5. What agreements did the delegates at Geneva make regarding Vietnam?

6. How did Ho strengthen his power in the territory north of the seventeenth parallel?

7. **Critical Thinking** Who would have been most happy with the Geneva Accords? Explain your answer.

CHAPTER 1 REVIEW

Vocabulary and People

Dean Acheson
Annam
assimilation
Bao Dai
Cao Dai
central highlands
coastal highlands
Cochinchina
cold war
collaborate
collectivization
containment
Dai Viet
Dienbienphu
domino theory
Paul Doumer
John Foster Dulles
Dwight D. Eisenhower
Paul Ely
Zhou Enlai
Charles De Gaulle
Geneva Conference
Gia-Long
Vo Nguyen Giap
Hoa Hao
Ho Chi Minh
imperialism
Indochinese Communist Party
Jacques Philippe Leclerc
Douglas MacArthur
Mekong Delta
Pierre Mendès-France
Minh Mang
Nam-Viet
Napoleon III
nationalist
Henri Navarre
northern highlands
partition
Pigneau de Béhaine
Potsdam Conference
puppet
quota
Red River Delta
Matthew Ridgway
seventeenth parallel
Tonkin
Harry S. Truman
Tu-Doc
Versailles Conference
Vietminh

Identification

Write the numbered sentence on a sheet of paper. In each sentence fill in the blank with one of these terms: *cold war, Dienbienphu, domino theory, imperialism, seventeenth parallel.*

1. Under the _____, if one country in Southeast Asia fell to the Communists, neighboring countries would soon follow suit.

2. French colonialism in Indochina ended with the defeat at _____.

3. Under the terms of the Geneva Conference, Vietnam was divided at the _____.

4. The _____ refers to the state of tension between Communist and non-Communist nations after World War II.

5. A country that takes over another country to gain economic and political advantages is said to be following a policy of _____.

Reviewing the Main Ideas

1. Why have the Vietnamese people historically feared the Chinese?

2. Describe the role played by religion in the French conquest of Vietnam.

3. What strains did French imperialism impose on Vietnamese society?

4. What opportunity did World War II offer the Vietnamese nationalists?

5. Describe the beginnings of American involvement in Vietnam.

Critical Thinking

As World War II came to an end, Emperor Bao Dai was named as "supreme adviser" to Ho Chi Minh's new government in Hanoi. He was thus able to observe the Vietminh in action, as he indicated in a letter to General De Gaulle. Read the excerpt from that letter and then answer the questions that follow:

> You would understand better if you could see what is happening here, if you could feel this yearning for independence that is in everyone's heart, and which no human force can any longer restrain. Should you re-establish a French administration here, it will not be obeyed. Every village will be a nest of resistance, each former collaborator an enemy, and your officials and colonists will themselves seek to leave this atmosphere, which will choke them.

THE HISTORY OF VIETNAM TO 1954

1. What does Bao Dai say will happen if the French try to return to Vietnam?

2. What would account for the "yearning for independence" that Bao Dai refers to?

3. Why do you think Ho Chi Minh chose to make Bao Dai his "supreme adviser"?

4. What do you think was General De Gaulle's reaction to Bao Dai's letter? Consider, for example, other advice the French leader was receiving at the time.

President Diem and family at his home in Hué.

CHAPTER TWO

AMERICA'S GROWING COMMITMENT

(1954–1963)

ON JUNE 26, 1954, A SHORT MAN DRESSED IN A WHITE linen suit stepped from a plane at Saigon's airport. Having spent the last four years in exile in the United States and Europe, he had been chosen to be prime minister of Vietnam by Emperor Bao Dai while the Geneva Conference was under way. He was hailed by a small crowd of Catholic supporters, numbering barely five hundred, and then was whisked away in a waiting car. The rest of Saigon, not knowing or not caring who he was, had stayed home.

While his welcome home may have been less than triumphant, **Ngo Dinh Diem** would soon make his mark on Vietnam. A courageous and dedicated nationalist who had opposed French rule, Diem was also a fervent anti–Communist. These qualities gained him the official, if hesitant, backing of the United States.

THE VIETNAM WAR

In this chapter, you will read how the United States, through its backing of Diem, became increasingly involved in Vietnam. As you read, look for answers to the following questions:

1. **How effective was Ngo Dinh Diem's leadership?**
2. **Why did John Kennedy step up American involvement in Vietnam?**
3. **Why was Diem overthrown?**

1 NGO DINH DIEM LEADS SOUTH VIETNAM

From the start, Diem's government in Saigon was plagued by uncertainty and internal instability. Diem had almost no experienced civil servants. He also had no base of support in the countryside. His army, finally, had been created by the French in the last months of the year, and, in the words of a French general, was nothing more than a "rabble."

The United States, reluctant to back a shaky regime, was eager that Diem demonstrate strong leadership. Eisenhower even told him that American aid would depend on his "standards of performance." Nevertheless, it was clear that, as Lyndon Johnson later put it, Diem was "the only boy we got out there."

Two Separate States The Geneva accords had established a truce between France and the Vietminh that was intended to be only temporary. The truce would be followed, it was assumed, by a lasting political solution. From the start, however, Ngo Dinh Diem rejected all agreements made in Geneva. Aware that Ho Chi Minh would handily win any national election, Diem had no intention of participating in his own downfall. In this, he had the backing of the United States (which privately estimated that Ho would win as much as 80 percent of the vote).

The election deadline, then, passed, and it looked as if Vietnam would be permanantly divided, like Germany and Korea. In the United Nations, the Soviet Union even proposed admitting the two states as **North Vietnam** and **South Vietnam**, "two separate states . . . which differ from one another in political and economic structure." The United States refused to consider such a proposal.

The French Departure No sooner had Diem arrived in Saigon in June, 1954, when rumors flew about a possible military

coup d'état (an effort to overthrow a government by force). General Nguyen Van Hinh, Diem's army chief of staff and a man with close ties to the French, had the support of the conniving Bao Dai as well as of the army. The coup was averted only at the last minute when Hinh was told that American aid would be cut off if Diem were ousted. Hihn later boasted that "nothing could have opposed the army.... I had only to lift my telephone and the coup d'état would have been over."

Many American and French observers believed that Diem faced a hopeless future, but in Washington, Secretary Dulles disagreed. He ordered $300 million in aid, believing that Diem only needed time to establish himself.

Dulles' decision angered Edgar Faure, the new French prime minister, who called Diem "not only incapable but mad." It led to a French pull-out from South Vietnam in 1956, one of Dulles' secret aims all along. On April 10, almost a century after the first French army had landed in Saigon, 10,000 soldiers of the French Expeditionary Corps marched through the South Vietnamese capital in a farewell parade. They were headed to another ill-fated colonial enterprise—the doomed effort to put down the revolution against French rule in Algeria.

Diem and the Private Armies The many political and religious factions offered Diem further challenges. When the Cao Dai and Hoa Hao (page 12) defied his government, he used American funds to bribe them into submission, paying out as much as $3 million to each sect. He then faced the **Binh Xuyen**, a powerful force of armed gangsters operating in Saigon. Their leader, Bay Vien, controlled the Saigon police and had grown wealthy through drug trafficking. He also had an army of 25,000 men at his disposal.

The power-hungry Binh Xuyen, with strong ties both to French elements still in the country as well as to Emperor Bao Dai, began firing on Diem's forces in March, 1955. Many observers predicted the end of Diem, but in a display of stubborn courage he came out fighting, directing all-out attacks on the Binh Xuyen. Fighting raged through Saigon for a month, with artillery and mortar fire destroying many of the city's poorer neighborhoods.

To the surprise of nearly everyone, Diem emerged victorious and was rewarded with a promise of full United States support. He would pay a price in the future, however, for some 2,000 of the defeated gang members fled to the Meking Delta where they joined underground Communist forces.

VIETNAM FACT

Just as his arch–rival Ho Chi Minh had once lived in the United States, so too did Ngo Dinh Diem. Fleeing a Vietminh death threat in 1950, the devout Diem spent two years at the Maryknoll Seminary in Lakewood, New Jersey. While living like a novice at Lakewood, he was able to arrange meetings with several leading American Catholics. Among them were Francis Cardinal Spellman of New York and Senator John F. Kennedy. During their talks, Diem would describe his opposition both to French colonization and Communist domination. The support he gained from these influential Americans would prove invaluable when he returned to Vietnam.

The End of Bao Dai After his amazing victory over the Binh Xuyen, Diem enjoyed a surge of popularity. Quickly, plans were made to oust Bao Dai and form a new government with Diem as chief of state. Bao Dai, who was living in France, tried to compete in the rigged elections that would decide his fate, but he had no real chance of victory. Though Diem surely would have won in an honest election, he claimed victory by the incredible margin of 98.2 percent. (In Saigon he received 605,000 votes, even though only 405,000 citizens were registered.) This was far more than the 60 percent margin his American advisers had told him "would look better."

A new constitution was also approved in October, 1955, giving the new president sweeping powers. He could override the decisions of the legislature in most matters and was given the right to deprive citizens of civil rights for "national security" reasons.

The Campaign Against the Communists After the Geneva Conference, some 120,000 Vietminh troops and supporters had moved north, expecting to return to their homes after the agreed-upon elections. Others had remained behind. Now, by early 1956, having defeated his opponents in Saigon, Diem turned against dissenters of every stripe, labeling them all as Communists.

Using much the same tactics as Ho, who was rooting out "landlords" and anti-Communist elements in the North (page 25), Diem's forces arrested anyone who had fought the French or who was even related to a former resistance member. As in the North, jealous neighbors or corrupt officials routinely denounced innocent people. Tried not in courts, but by "security committees" under Diem's control, prisoners were often tortured.

By the end of 1956, the remnants of the Vietminh had been crushed. Few survived, and those who did retreated into remote areas, far from the police and informers who watched every village. Eventually, those veterans would join with other anti–Diem elements to form the **National Liberation Front (NLF)**. Although quickly dominated by Communists, in its early years the Central Committee of the NLF reflected the diverse groups under its banner, and included several Buddhists monks, Bao Dai supporters, a Catholic priest, and a montagnard chief. The Diem government mockingly called them the **Vietcong**, a name which stuck.

So complete was Diem's apparent triumph, that in 1957 he paid a state visit to the United States, where he was greeted enthusiastically. He was at a point where he might have created a strong, unified nation. But the way he governed and key mistakes that he made in the next few years sealed his fate.

Diem's Inner Circle Power in the South Vietnamese government rested firmly in the hands of Diem's family. His four brothers, Can, Luyen, Thuc, and Nhu, and his sister–in–law, Madame Nhu, formed a powerful and corrupt political circle.

Can controlled central Vietnam, the Ngo family's ancestral home, which he ruled as a virtual warlord. He regularly extorted money from area businesses, executed enemies, and spread fear through mass arrests. Greedy like all the Ngos, he made his money operating a smuggling ring that sold opium in Hué and shipped rice to North Vietnam. Luyen, another brother, was an ambassador and a kind of international spokesman for the regime. He made a fortune in currency exchange manipulations. Thuc, meanwhile, was archbishop of Hué, a position he used to his own advantage. He bought apartment buildings, rubber estates, and timber concessions, and took part in shady land deals. He was instrumental in helping his brother's regime gain Catholic support, at home and abroad.

The most influential of Diem's brothers, **Ngo Dinh Nhu**, served as the president's closest political adviser. Suspicious of everyone, he ran his own semisecret political party, members of which were carefully placed in top government posts. There they spied on fellow workers, reporting directly to Nhu about any potential trouble–makers or opponents of the regime. Vain and arrogant, Nhu became a symbol of the Diem regime. In his last years, most observers were sure that Nhu was a drug addict and that opium and heroin had caused him to loose his grip on reality.

The public soon became aware of the Diem family's power. It was apparent that the legislature, the courts, the political parties were in place mainly to please Western opinion, not to advance democracy. The real power, the real government was found in the presidential palace and there alone.

Absence of Land Reform Allied to Diem's inner circle were wealthy landowners, most of whom lived in Saigon. He allowed them to retain large holdings, even when the influx of northern refugees dramatized the need for land reform. To make matters worse, he forced peasants to pay for land that the Vietminh had given them free during the war against France.

As Communist activity picked up in the late 1950's, Diem further angered peasant farmers by creating **agrovilles.** These farm communities, later known as **strategic hamlets,** were designed to protect rural inhabitants from Communist attacks. But the peasants had to leave their native villages and the sites of their ancestral graves for overcrowded, dirty camps where little schooling, medical care, or other social services were provided, and where corrupt government officials ruled despotically. The peasants especially objected to the forced labor necessary to build the camps.

The contrast with the Vietcong's land distribution program made a strong impression on the peasants too. Once a village had fallen under Communist control, the land of rich landlords was confiscated and distributed to poor peasants at no cost. Absentee landlords lost their land as well, their properties being parceled out to the tenants who worked it. Although remaining committed to the goal of collectivization (page 25), the Communists were willing for the time being to permit private ownership of land as a means of gaining peasant support.

Another mistake Diem made in the countryside was to replace all previously elected village chiefs and village councils with hand-picked outsiders. A saying—"the emperor's law stops at the village gate"—had always been honored in Vietnam. Even the French had treated Vietnam's villages as self-governing units with their own elected officials. Now, in his move to establish absolute control, Diem further angered the peasants. A captured guerrilla compared the peasants to a "mound of straw ready to be ignited."

Middle-Class Opposition Along with rising peasant discontent was growing opposition in the towns and cities. Led by teachers, doctors, and other professionals, urban dissatisfaction was heightened in August, 1959, when Diem organized legislative elections.

Held mainly to show the United States that Western-style democracy had taken hold in South Vietnam, the elections were blatantly dishonest. In one noted case, a government opponent won election to the National Assembly by a six-to-one margin, but was disqualified on the grounds that during the campaign he had made too many speeches. When political opponents, including several former members of his Cabinet, pleaded for reform, Diem accused them of "Communist affiliations." He closed opposition newspapers and threw a number of prominent critics in jail.

The role of the Americans confused many middle-class Vietnamese. While welcoming outside help in the fight against the Vietcong, educated people found American support of Diem to be hypocritical. Particularly disturbing was advice given by Frederick Nolting, the United States ambassador to South Vietnam. Addressing the Saigon Rotary club in February, 1962, Nolting advised, "What a marvelous transformation would take place in this country if all those who criticize their government would decide to work with it and for it."

Middle-class opponents also chafed under Diem's morality campaigns. Prodded by his sister-in-law, Madame Nhu, Diem closed Saigon's nightclubs and ballrooms, and banned beauty contests and boxing matches. Cafés were allowed to remain open, but only if the bar girls, many of them prostitutes, wore long white blouses. These and other defenses of what Madame Nhu called Vietnam's "traditional virtues" exasperated the Vietnamese, who were well aware of the Ngos' corruption.

American Anxiety By 1960, with opposition to Diem rising, the United States was growing concerned. Already it had sunk more than $1 billion in backing Diem. In addition, there were more than 1,500 Americans in South Vietnam, helping the government in various ways. Still, Diem disregarded American pleas for land reform, ignored economic development, and seemed interested only in preserving his own power. Remaining suspicious of foreign interference, he found an effective technique—when dealing with American advisers he simply did all the talking himself, going on for six, seven, even ten hours. Some viewed his compulsive talking as a serious psychiatric problem. Because of his firm anti-Communist stand, however, he remained capable of manipulating the United States. He was, in the words of one American official, "a puppet who pulls his own strings."

American anxiety heightened in November, 1960, when

THE VIETNAM WAR

troops led by Vuong Van Dong, an idealistic young lieutenant colonel, surrounded the presidential palace and demanded reforms in government. Diem outwitted the soldiers by stalling for time and, in a radio speech, promising to hold free elections. Loyal troops then arrived on the scene and crushed the revolt. Dong fled to Cambodia, while Diem rounded up more critics and went back on his election promises. From then on, however, plots against him grew more numerous. Seeing enemies everywhere, Diem became more and more isolated, relying only on his family. He also refused to permit any troop movements without his personal approval, crippling the military campaign against the Vietcong.

SECTION 1 REVIEW

1. **Vocabulary to Know** coup d'état, North Vietnam, South Vietnam, National Liberation Front (NLF), Vietcong, agroville, strategic hamlet

2. **People to Identify** Ngo Dinh Diem, Binh Xuyen, Ngo Dinh Nhu, Madame Nhu

3. What was Diem's view of the Geneva accords?

4. Why did the French leave South Vietnam?

5. What was the result of Diem's struggle with the private armies?

6. What role did Diem's family play in governing South Vietnam?

7. **Critical Thinking** Why did opposition to Diem rise among the peasants? Among middle-class city dwellers?

2 JOHN KENNEDY STEPS UP AMERICAN INVOLVEMENT

Until 1959, Ho Chi Minh, who was tightening his control of North Vietnam, warned his southern followers about "reckless" attacks against the Diem regime. With Diem's forces threatening to wipe out the southern Communists, however, Ho issued new orders, authorizing "armed struggle." Immediately, a brutal assassination campaign against pro-government village chiefs and officials was begun. An observer to the murder of two police officers described a typical scene:

They forced the two men to kneel by the roadside, and one of the Vietcong guys chopped off their heads with a machete. They then pinned verdicts to their shirts saying that the murdered men were policemen. The verdicts had been written out beforehand. It was horrible to watch.

Between 1959 and 1961 the number of murdered officials soared from 1,200 to 4,000 a year. The new administration in Washington, led by **John F. Kennedy**, watched with concern and debated the direction American policy should take.

Kennedy and Foreign Policy After being sworn in as President on January 19, 1961, John Kennedy issued a challenge to the American people and a warning to the rest of the world. Americans, he promised, would "pay any price, bear any burden, meet any hardship, support any friend, oppose any foe to assure the survival and success of liberty." Were these dramatic words to be taken literally, particularly when policymakers faced a perplexing situation like Vietnam? Throughout his short term of office, even as America's commitment to South Vietnam continued to grow, Kennedy would give contradictory signals about his intentions.

Certainly, Kennedy had supported Diem's regime from the beginning. A firm believer in containment, he had once described South Vietnam as "the cornerstone of the Free World in Southeast Asia" and a "test of American responsibility and determination." To abandon Diem to the Communists, he asserted, would be a prelude to losing our national security "piece by piece, country by country."

Yet for all his fine words, Kennedy was not really prepared to "pay any price" to defend South Vietnam. Other, more pressing issues would occupy him from the start—the Bay of Pigs fiasco, the Berlin crisis, a summit meeting in Vienna with Soviet Prime Minister Khrushchev, even the fighting between Communist and government forces in neighboring Laos.[1] Kennedy regarded Vietnam as a problem that could be dealt with inexpensively, one that should not be allowed to become a major concern. He rejected abandoning Vietnam, but he could never accept the idea of fighting a major war there. Kennedy's middle path was, however, dangerous. It encouraged Diem to ignore outside advice, while leading Americans to believe that they could play a limited role without having to pay a heavy price.

[1.] The crisis in Laos was temporarily resolved in 1962 with the installation of a neutralist coalition government.

Cabinet Officers and Advisers Key aides would play crucial roles in shaping America's Vietnam policy in the years to come. For his Secretary of State, Kennedy named **Dean Rusk,** a soft-spoken Georgian who had long viewed the Vietnam conflict in cold war terms. In 1950, while Assistant Secretary of State for Far Eastern affairs in the Truman administration, he had told the Senate Foreign Relations Committee, "This is a civil war that has been in effect captured by the [Soviet] Politburo and, besides, has been turned into a tool of the Politburo. So it isn't a civil war in the usual sense. It is part of an international war." Nothing in the intervening years had caused Rusk to change that view.

For Secretary of Defense, Kennedy chose **Robert S. McNamara.** As a top executive of the Ford Motor Company, McNamara had gained a reputation for finding efficient ways to produce desired results. He would approach Vietnam almost as if it too were a business problem that could be solved through precise, rational approaches.

Rusk and McNamara agreed that an aggressive response was required in the face of the stepped-up Communist activity in South Vietnam. They were backed by **Walt Rostow,** a leading State Department official, and by **Maxwell Taylor.** A handsome World War II hero who was said to be Kennedy's favorite general, Taylor would serve as chairman of the Joint Chiefs of Staff from 1962 to 1964.

Flexible Response It was Taylor, in fact, whose recommendations in 1961 regarding a deeper American commitment to Vietnam greatly influenced the President. Kennedy had never been happy with the Eisenhower administration's policy of **massive retaliation** (a strategy calling for all-out military action against an aggressor nation). Taylor advocated **flexible response** as a way of dealing with guerrilla warfare. Under this approach, specially trained advisers would teach local forces antiguerrilla, or "counterinsurgency," methods. Soon, Americans would be at work in every phase of South Vietnamese military operations.

Immediately, programs were beefed up at the Special Warfare Center at Fort Bragg. The men of the U.S. Army Special Forces, nicknamed **Green Berets** because of the distinctive green berets they wore, were trained in methods of fighting guerrillas in the jungles and mountains of the Third World. The Green Berets became great favorites of Kennedy, serving almost to symbolize his administration's vigorous, "can–do" image. The youthful President was so fascinated by them that he would observe their training sessions and once invited a unit of them to the grounds of the Kennedy family home on Cape Cod to demonstrate their skills.

AMERICA'S GROWING COMMITMENT (1954-1963)

In April, 1961, Kennedy agreed to send an additional 100 American military advisers to Vietnam—bringing the total to nearly 800. Their task was to strengthen the **Army of the Republic of Vietnam (ARVN)** by 20,000 men. This decision, however, violated the Geneva accords, which stated that no new foreign military personnel could enter Vietnam unless as replacements. Rusk, aware of the violation, suggested that the Americans "be placed in various locations to avoid attention."

Diem had misgivings about allowing the additional American advisers into South Vietnam. He opposed any move that would give outsiders influence over his government. But soon the American presence would grow much larger.

Troop Build-Up In May, 1961, Kennedy sent his Vice President, **Lyndon Johnson,** on a goodwill trip through Asia. During Johnson's stop in Vietnam, where he called Diem the "Winston Churchill of Asia," the question of raising South Vietnam's troop strength from 100,000 to 270,000 men was discussed. Such an increase would have required large numbers of American advisers and additional sums of money. Diem at first hesitated, but in the next few months Vietcong attacks mounted sharply as former Vietminh guerrillas began making their way back south.

Well prepared, combat tough, and homesick, most of the returnees made the long trek into South Vietnam along the **Ho Chi Minh Trail.** Not a single trail but, rather, a network of paths, the Ho Chi Minh Trail was North Vietnam's lifeline to the Communists fighting in the South. An American who observed the trail while hiding in the Laotian jungle in 1964 described it as "a highway. Next a foot trail. Then a bicycle path." He went on to say:

> I never saw a truck, but I heard them in the jungle and saw the tracks. They'd drive their trucks as far as they could. Carriers would offload the trucks, throw the goods in homemade rucksacks, go x more [kilometers] on down the trail, and they'd have to climb, but the steps were already built into the mountain. They'd pass their stuff onto bicycles, rigged their saddlebags with something like a yoke across the front so they could steer the bike as they pushed it.

Maxwell Taylor, on a two-week tour of Vietnam, was aware of the Communist movement south and favored an increased American presence. In an "eyes-only" message for the President, he proposed sending 8,000 combat troops to South Vietnam as well as three squadrons of helicopters.

Debate swirled through the administration, as McNamara and the Joint Chiefs rejected Taylor's proposal, urging instead that the President deploy 200,000 Americans. Kennedy was clearly not prepared to order such a large force to Vietnam. Advised by General Douglas MacArthur (page 12) against involving the United States in another land war in Asia, he persuaded McNamara to postpone any decision on troops while increasing aid to Diem.

In spite of Kennedy's caution, over the next two years more and more American advisers were sent to prop up the Diem regime. There were more than 9,000 advisers in Vietnam by the end of 1962. By November, 1963, at the time of Kennedy's assassination, the figure had climbed to over 16,000. In addition, by that time Americans were secretly involved in combat. Advisers often accompanied ARVN units on combat missions. Helicopter pilots were assigned to drop detachments of ARVN troops into battle zones and then to pick up the dead and wounded. Americans also flew with the Vietnamese on bombing missions, and if there were not enough pilots, the Americans would take the planes out themselves. By the time of Kennedy's death, American pilots in Vietnam had flown some 7,000 air sorties, lost 23 aircraft, and suffered the deaths of 108 men.

Kennedy and Public Opinion Americans were dying in Vietnam in combat, but this fact was carefully kept from the American people. For instance, at a press conference in 1962 Kennedy was directly asked if United States troops were fighting in Vietnam. His one-word answer: "No." Not wanting to acknowledge that a war was really being fought, however, the President could not impose censorship on the news media. For the time being, administration figures tried to get journalists to present a positive view of the American role.

What little the public heard about Vietnam was that victory was certain. After 48 hours in the country in 1962, Secretary McNamara concluded that "we are winning the war." In that same year Robert Kennedy, brother of the President, declared in Saigon, "we are going to win." In the words of one journalist, "The only two exports of South Vietnam are rice and American optimism."

The missionary zeal with which Americans approached the task before them, combined with the emphasis on rosy reports, often flew in the face of reality. But no matter. In the words of

General Paul Harkins, head of the American military assistance program in South Vietnam, "I am an optimist, and I am not going to allow my staff to be pessimistic."

The Introduction of Helicopters The rapid influx of troops and military equipment momentarily tipped the scales in the rapidly escalating war with the Vietcong in Diem's favor. Of that equipment, nothing made more of a difference than American helicopters.

The adaptable and effective helicopter would soon become a symbol of the Vietnam War. At first, choppers were used to carry ARVN troops and supplies into action or to haul wounded soldiers to medical tents or hospitals. Then, with the arrival of the UH-1 helicopters, or "Hueys," choppers began being used as assault weapons in support of ground troops.

In time, the Vietcong adapted to the helicopters. They dug shelters against helicopter raids and, as they acquired more sophisticated weapons, learned to knock them out of the sky. The helicopters also had a harmful effect on the South Vietnamese war effort. Diem became more reluctant to attack the Vietcong head-on, preferring instead to call in American air strikes. His aim more and more was to protect himself against possible trouble in Saigon. To do that, he did not want to lose men fighting the Vietcong.

SECTION 2 REVIEW

1. **Vocabulary to Know** massive retaliation, flexible response, Green Berets, Army of the Republic of Vietnam (ARVN), Ho Chi Minh Trail

2. **People to Identify** John F. Kennedy, Dean Rusk, Robert S. McNamara, Walt Rostow, Maxwell Taylor, Lyndon Johnson

3. What did Kennedy's top aides think the role of the United States should be in South Vietnam?

4. (a) Why were American military advisers sent to South Vietnam? (b) How did their duties expand as time went by?

5. How many American advisers were in South Vietnam by the time of Kennedy's assassination?

6. **Critical Thinking** What are the dangers in an over-emphasis on optimism?

3 DIEM IS OVERTHROWN

Ngo Dinh Diem was able to stay in power for nine years, playing off South Vietnam's turbulent religious and political factions against each other and clamping down hard on the opposition. In so doing, however, he turned nearly everyone in his nation against him, and he ended by being forced from power and murdered.

Buddhist Opposition An unlikely event marked the beginning of the end for Diem. On May 8, 1963, at a celebration in Hué of the 2,527th birthday of the Buddha, a Catholic official prohibited the city's Buddhists from flying their flag. Angered because the papal colors had been displayed at a Catholic celebration the week before, several thousand people marched peacefully to the city's radio station. When armed troops arrived on the scene, the demonstrators refused to leave. The soldiers opened fire and eight children and a woman died, either from gunfire or from being trampled to death.

The Buddhists had long been persecuted in Vietnam, particularly under the French. Catholicism was given a special place in society. The Buddhists charged that little had changed under the Catholic Diem. They complained that Catholics received the best government jobs, were favored in army promotions, and enjoyed other advantages. They even feared that Madame Nhu's anti-vice campaign was an effort to make Catholicism the nation's official religion. The resentment of South Vietnam's 10.5 million Buddhists, then, had long been simmering beneath the surface, ready to explode.

Following the Hué incident, Buddhist organizations went into action, stirring up hatred of Diem. As protests spread, the United States grew concerned. Ambassador Nolting urged Diem to talk with the Buddhists, but Diem refused any suggestion of conciliation. Madame Nhu added to the crisis by charging wildly that the Americans were behind the Buddhist protests.

Suicide by Fire The stubborn Diem refused to talk even after a startling event made world headlines. On July 11, 1963, an elderly Buddhist monk named Quang Duc sat down in a busy Saigon intersection. As shocked pedestrians looked on, other monks and nuns encircled him. One poured gasoline over his body and another ignited him with a lighter. A flash of fire leaped up, and Quang Duc burned to death in grisly protest to Diem.

In the weeks that followed, more Buddhist monks went up in

AMERICA'S GROWING COMMITMENT (1954-1963)

flames, sparking further demonstations. American officials grew anxious, yet their requests for reform were ignored.

A New American Ambassador With the enormous sums of money provided South Vietnam by the United States, the American ambassador in Saigon wielded great power and influence. The appointment of a new ambassador in June, 1963, then, was of more than passing interest. It signalled a change in official American policy toward the Diem regime.

Henry Cabot Lodge was in some ways a surprising choice as ambassador. Not only was he a prominent Republican, but he had been defeated twice by John Kennedy in electoral contests.[2] Still, having recently served as a vigorous ambassador to the United Nations, Lodge shared the view of many top administration figures that the United States had put up with Diem for too long and that he was harming the effort to defeat the Vietcong.

No sooner was Lodge's appointment announced than discussions about overthrowing Diem were held. In Washington, Kennedy and his aides debated the likelihood of a coup. In Saigon, generals offended by Diem's policies or simply greedy for power began making plans of their own.

The Attack on the Pagodas In the middle of August, Frederick Nolting left Saigon, still proclaiming his backing of Diem and even claiming that he had "never seen any evidence of religious persecution" during his two years as ambassador to South Vietnam. A week later, Diem imposed **martial law** (rule by military authorites) and made plans for a move against the Buddhists.

Diem's plan, designed by his brother Nhu, was typically complicated and marked by intrigue. He would use loyal troops disguised as regular army forces in attacks against the Buddhists. If the plan worked, he would not only have cracked down on the Buddhists, but would have turned their wrath against the army, which he suspected of plotting against him. So complete were Nhu's preparations that he ordered the telephone lines to the United States embassy cut, so that American officials would also be tricked into believing the regular army was leading the attacks.

On the night of August 21, Nhu's men struck. In Saigon, they attacked the city's main **pagoda** (a Buddhist house of worship), lobbing tear gas grenades into the temple before dragging their captives into army trucks. In Hué they laid siege to a hastily

---

[2.] Kennedy had taken Lodge's Massachusetts Senate seat in 1952. In 1960 Lodge was Richard Nixon's running mate on the losing Republican ticket.

barricaded sanctuary, finally clearing a way through its furious defenders with armored cars. Throughout the country they raided some 2,000 pagodas and rounded up more than 1,400 Buddhists. Several hundred people may have been killed.

Coup Plans Within days, Nhu's direction of the brutal raids had been revealed, and the country erupted in protest. Students boycotted classes while government officials resigned their posts. In one embarrassing move, Tran Van Chuong, Madame Nhu's father and ambassador to the United States, resigned and denounced the Diem regime. Now the country was united as never before against the Ngos.

The United States too had turned against Diem. Ambassador Lodge, aware that South Vietnamese army officers were making plans to overthrow Diem, pleaded for swift American backing for such a venture. Fearful that South Vietnam might soon fall to the Communists, Lodge knew the plotters would not move unless they received a positive signal from the Americans. In a cable to Washington, Lodge underlined the seriousness of the situation:

> We are launched on a course from which there is no responsible turning back: the overthrow of the Diem government. There is no turning back because U.S. prestige is already publicly committed to this end in large measure, and will become more so as the facts leak out. In a more fundamental sense, there is no turning back because there is no possibility, in my view, that the war can be won under a Diem administration.

Kennedy gave Lodge strong backing, even allowing his ambassador to suspend American aid to Diem. In an interview on CBS television, Kennedy suggested that the Diem regime had "gotten out of touch with the people." While not prepared to withdraw from Vietnam, Kennedy noted that "[I]n the final analysis it is their war. They are the ones who have to win it or lose it. We can help them ... but they have to win it—the people of Vietnam."

American Backing To Lodge's dismay the conspiring officers grew suddenly hesitant, suspecting betrayal. They also feared that they lacked the strength to bring Diem down. Not until early October did they again begin making coup plans. Led by **Duong Van Minh**—known, because of his bulk, as "Big" Minh—the army officers wanted a promise that the Americans would "not thwart" any coup. They also wanted a pledge that American aid would resume after Diem's downfall.

The generals got what they wanted. In a cable to Lodge, Kennedy wrote, "While we do not wish to stimulate a coup, we also do not wish to leave the impression that the United States would thwart a change of government." A few days later, the generals were told of the President's decision.

The Fall of Diem On November 1, 1963, rebel troops circled the presidential palace, while others quickly occupied the radio station and police headquarters. Diem and Nhu, barricaded in the palace's cellar, called for loyal troops to save them, but no one responded. Realizing their desperate situation, the brothers made a dramatic get-away, leaving their unknowing guards behind to die defending the palace.

Slipping into a waiting Land Rover, Diem and Nhu drove through the deserted city to a hide-out in Cholon, the Chinese section of Saigon. The next morning Diem called "Big" Minh, asking to negotiate. When the offer was refused, Diem agreed to turn himself over to the generals at Saint Francis Xavier, a French church in Cholon.

Troops were sent to the church to pick up Diem and Nhu. Before they left they were ordered—probably by Minh—to kill both their prisoners. Once Diem and Nhu had been locked inside an armored car, they were shot and stabbed repeatedly.

For the time being, Saigon welcomed the news of Diem's downfall. Cheering crowds smashed statues of Diem, showered ARVN troops with flowers, and cheered as political prisoners were set free and as nightclubs re-opened. In the countryside, peasants ransacked the hated strategic hamlets. Americans, viewed as having engineered the coup, were cheered wherever they went. Lodge, now looking forward to a shorter war against the Vietcong, invited the victorious generals to the American embassy to congratulate them. The future looked bright.

SECTION 3 REVIEW

1. **Vocabulary to Know** martial law, pagoda

2. **People to Identify** Henry Cabot Lodge, Duong Van Minh

3. What event set off Buddhist protests against Diem's regime?

4. Why did Diem order attacks on the Buddhist pagodas?

5. **Critical Thinking** What role did the United States play in the coup against Diem?

CHAPTER 2 REVIEW

Vocabulary and People

agroville
Army of the Republic of
  Vietnam (ARVN)
coup d'état
Ngo Dinh Diem
flexible response
Green Beret
Ho Chi Minh Trail
Lyndon Johnson
John F. Kennedy
Henry Cabot Lodge
Robert S. McNamara
martial law
massive retaliation

Duong Van Minh
National Liberation
  Front (NLF)
Madame Nhu
Ngo Dinh Nhu
North Vietnam
pagoda
Walt Rostow
Dean Rusk
South Vietnam
strategic hamlet
Maxwell Taylor
Binh Xuyen

Identification

On a separate sheet of paper, write the term from the column on the right that best matches the phrase on the left.

1. Name given to Communist forces in South Vietnam.

2. President of South Vietnam.

3. Influential Chairman of the Joint Chiefs of Staff who urged a policy of flexible retaliation.

4. American military forces specially trained in antiguerrilla warfare.

5. American ambassador involved in plot against the South Vietnamese government.

A. Green Berets

B. Ngo Dinh Diem

C. Henry Cabot Lodge

D. Maxwell Taylor

E. Vietcong

AMERICA'S GROWING COMMITMENT (1954-1963)

Reviewing the Main Ideas

1. Why did Ngo Dinh Diem surprise most observers during his first years in power?

2. Why was Diem called "a puppet who pulls his own strings"?

3. For what reasons did Communist attacks mount in the late 1950's?

4. What factors contributed to Diem's downfall?

5. What was the extent of American involvement in Vietnam by 1963?

Critical Thinking

In 1962, Mike Mansfield, the new Senate Majority Leader, submitted a private report on Vietnam to President Kennedy. Read the following excerpt from that report and then answer the questions that follow:

> Vietnam, outside the cities, is still an insecure place which is run at night largely by the Vietcong. The government in Saigon is still seeking acceptance by the ordinary people in large areas of the countryside. Out of fear or indifference or hostility the peasants are still without acquiescence [passive support], let alone approval of that government.

1. What did Senator Mansfield have to say about the strength of the Vietcong?

2. Would you describe the tone of the report as optimistic or pessimistic? Explain your answer.

3. Kennedy was reported to be furious when he read what Mansfield had to say. Why do you suppose he had that reaction?

49

Troops aboard the USNS Gen. Le Roy Eltinge July 29, 1965.

CHAPTER THREE

THE FIGHTING INTENSIFIES

(1963–1967)

ON NOVEMBER 23, 1963, JOHN KENNEDY WAS assassinated in Dallas and Lyndon Johnson succeeded to the presidency. Johnson did not enter the Oval Office eager to confront Ho Chi Minh. Wanting to spend all his energies on his domestic program—later called the Great Society—and painfully inexperienced in foreign affairs, Johnson was nevertheless confronted from the start with the situation in Vietnam. He knew that any sign of weakness would result in attacks from the political right. He recalled only too well the damage done to Harry Truman's presidency when Senator Joseph McCarthy and others charged that the Democrats had "lost" China to the Communists in 1949. So Johnson could not wish Vietnam away, as he so plainly desired. For as long as he could, though, Johnson would divert the nation's attention from Southeast Asia, denying even that America was on the verge of going to war there.

In this chapter you will read how the United States became fully involved in the war in Vietnam. As you read, look for answers to the following questions:

1. Why did Lyndon Johnson try to ignore the situation in Vietnam?
2. Under what circumstances did Congress pass the Gulf of Tonkin Resolution?
3. How did the United States become fully involved in the Vietnam War?

1 LYNDON JOHNSON TRIES TO IGNORE THE SITUATION IN VIETNAM

Looking back on his presidency, Lyndon Johnson would later admit that "Losing the Great Society was a terrible thought, but not so terrible as the thought of being responsible for America's losing a war to the Communists. Nothing would be worse than that." This, then, was Johnson's dilemma—and one he faced from the start.

A Deteriorating Situation In the short time since the assassination both of Presidents Diem and Kennedy, the prospects of the new South Vietnamese government had grown bleak indeed. Administrators loyal to Diem had been replaced with cronies of the generals, and most were worse than their predecessors. In Saigon, a military council supposedly ruled the country, but its twelve members quarreled and plotted constantly, accomplishing nothing. General Minh, the coup leader (page 46), preferred playing tennis to governing, and he was overthrown in January, 1965, by another general, **Nguyen Khanh.** Khanh proved to be just as incompetent. As if to symbolize his shaky leadership, he took up residence in a house on the Saigon River from which he could quickly flee by boat if necessary.

Former optimists in Washington sensed trouble. Secretary of Defense McNamara, like most of the major foreign policy figures in the Kennedy administration, had been kept on by Johnson. After a quick trip to Saigon late in 1963, he privately told Johnson that there would be a Communist victory within two or three months.

Soon, debate swirled over American policy. The Joint Chiefs of Staff called for forceful action. General Curtis LeMay, commander of the air force, called for the bombing of North Vietnam,

THE FIGHTING INTENSIFIES (1963-1967)

saying that "we are swatting flies when we should be going after the manure pile."

Such action, though later adopted, seemed too drastic for Johnson in 1964. Besides, in the upcoming presidential election he intended to run as a peace candidate. For the time being, he told the Joint Chiefs at a White House reception late in 1963, "Just get me elected, and then you can have your war."

North Vietnamese Plans As the new administration took charge in Washington, Ho Chi Minh and his top advisers watched from afar. It quickly became evident to them that the United States intended to remain in South Vietnam. As a result, the North Vietnamese made new plans.

Until 1963, most of the combat in the South had been carried on by veterans of the fight against the French who had gone north after the Geneva agreement and had later returned to their homes in the South. Their ranks, however, had been seriously weakened, and now Ho Chi Minh made a crucial decision. To ease their manpower and supply problems, the Vietcong began to rely more on force and terror. Young peasants were kidnapped and pressed into service. Farmers were made to contribute as much as a half of their income to the rebel cause.

A second key decision was to begin sending large detachments of North Vietnamese units south along the Ho Chi Minh Trail (page 41). By the end of 1964, as many as 10,000 North Vietnamese troops had gone south—and they were but a trickle compared to the numbers that would soon follow.

More American Aid Meanwhile, the United States responded to the situation in Vietnam as it had done in the past: by sending more aid. With General Khanh in power, however, little progress was possible. Khanh was known as a trouble-maker and as lacking in principle. In his career he had supported both the Vietminh and the French, and he had worked both for and against Diem. Now, in 1964, he adopted a strong anti-Communist stance, one he calculated would guarantee American support. He was right.

To demonstrate its backing of the new Saigon government, the Johnson administration sent Secretary McNamara back to South Vietnam in March, 1964. In a bizarre public relations campaign, McNamara and U.S. Chief of Staff Maxwell Taylor accompanied Khanh in American-style campaign appearances throughout the country. Heavily protected by government troops, McNamara would stiffly call out *"Vietnam moun man"* ("Vietnam a thousand years") to the crowds. Because of mistaken pronounciation, what he said often sounded to Vietnamese audiences like "Southern duck wants to lie down."

Beyond McNamara's pronouncements, the sight of a South Vietnamese head of state being escorted by his American backers was an affront to Vietnamese pride and nationalism. Khanh, however, benefited from the relationship. American economic assistance had been boosted by $50 million and the number of advisers had grown to 23,300. In April, Johnson told Lodge, "As far as I am concerned, you must have whatever you need to help the Vietnamese do the job." Still, the troubling fact remained that by the spring of 1964, the Vietcong controlled more than 40 percent of South Vietnam and more than 50 percent of its people.

The American Campaign for President in 1964 Unlike the phony campaigning with General Khanh, a real electoral contest was fast approaching in the United States. An accidental President, Johnson craved election in his own right—and he wanted to win big. The Republicans, meanwhile, were making preparations of their own.

In June, 1964, Ambassador Lodge resigned his post to seek the Republican nomination. Several prominent administration figures volunteered to replace Lodge, including Rusk, McNamara, and Robert Kennedy.[1] To please the military, Johnson selected Maxwell Taylor (page 40). In addition, he named **William Westmoreland** as the new commander of American forces in South Vietnam.

Although he had some early successes in the primaries, Lodge was not able to overcome the leading Republican candidate for President, Senator **Barry Goldwater** of Arizona. Perhaps the nation's best-known conservative spokesman, Goldwater was nominated by a wide margin at the party convention in San Francisco. He thrilled the delegates with his famous words "Extremism in the defense of liberty is no vice."

Goldwater did his best to draw the nation's attention to Vietnam, charging that there was a war going on there and that the United States was not doing enough to win it. But Johnson shrewdly prevented the war from becoming a major issue. He played on the public's fear that Goldwater was an extremist who might plunge the nation into nuclear war. Johnson also pledged that "We are not about to send American boys nine or ten thousand miles away from home to do what Asian boys ought to be doing for themselves." His restraint was such that when the

---

[1] In a note to Johnson, Kennedy wrote that Vietnam was "obviously the most important problem facing the United States and . . . I am at your service."

THE FIGHTING INTENSIFIES (1963-1967)

Vietcong attacked the Bien Hoa airfield (fifteen miles north of Saigon) two days before the election, killing four Americans and destroying or damaging thirteen planes, he declined to retaliate.

On Election Day, Johnson swept to a lopsided victory, capturing 61 percent of the popular vote. It was the largest majority in history until that time. Swept into office with him were huge Democratic majorities in both houses of Congress. The triumphant Johnson was at the height of his popularity.

SECTION 1 REVIEW

1. **People to Identify** Nguyen Khanh, William Westmoreland, Barry Goldwater

2. What was the situation in Vietnam at the time Lyndon Johnson became President?

3. How did the United States support the government of General Khanh?

4. (a) Who were the candidates for President in the election of 1964? (b) What was the outcome?

5. **Critical Thinking** Why did Johnson want to ignore the situation in Vietnam?

2 CONGRESS PASSES THE GULF OF TONKIN RESOLUTION

Under the Constitution, the President serves as commander in chief, while Congress alone has the power to declare war. This separation of power was respected by America's early Presidents, who obtained congressional approval for military actions. In time, though, Chief Executives gradually took from Congress most powers in foreign affairs. William McKinley sent troops to China to put down the Boxer Rebellion without consulting Congress. Woodrow Wilson followed suit in the Caribbean and Mexico. In more recent times, Harry Truman sent American forces to Korea without having Congress declare war.

Lyndon Johnson expected to act with similar authority in managing the Vietnam situation. Still, as the American presence in Southeast Asia grew larger, Johnson saw advantages in getting approval from Congress for his policies. In the summer of 1964 he secretly had his advisers come up with the draft of a congressional resolution. The resolution would give him the right to commit American forces to the defense of any Southeast Asian nation threatened by "aggression or subversion." The President alone would decide the seriousness of the threat.

Covert Activity Throughout 1964, Johnson denied that the United States was involved in any **covert,** or secret, activity in Vietnam. Nonetheless, Green Beret teams flew in and out of combat areas, the bombing of Laos near the North Vietnamese border was begun, and helicopters dropped South Vietnamese and U.S. commandos into waters off the North Vietnamese coast where they swam ashore and carried out secret missions of sabotage. In a move that would soon have lasting significance, Johnson also authorized hit-and-run raids by South Vietnamese PT boats against North Vietnamese naval bases. United States navy destroyers would back up the South Vietnamese by gathering "intelligence information."

Confrontation in the Gulf of Tonkin On July 31, 1964, four South Vietnamese PT boats attacked North Vietnamese naval bases on islands in the **Gulf of Tonkin,** the large, placid body of water along North Vietnam's coast. Trying to monitor the North Vietnamese naval installations, the United States destroyer *Maddox,* fitted with special electronic eavesdropping equipment, had been assigned to the area. The North Vietnamese assumed that the *Maddox* was a part of the same hostile operation, and on August 2 three North Vietnamese PT boats attacked the American vessel. The PT boats managed to get within two miles and fire one off-target torpedo before the Maddox sank one of the boats and crippled the two others.

The next day, the *Maddox* returned to patrol duty in the Gulf of Tonkin, accompanied by the *C. Turner Joy,* another destroyer. The commander of the Tonkin Gulf patrol, Captain John Herrick, anticipated trouble and cabled Washington, nervously suggesting that the patrol would be open to "unacceptable risk." Johnson, however, ordered the Americans to proceed and to "attack any force that attacks them." Additional fighter bombers were rushed to South Vietnam, and American combat troops were placed on alert. A confrontation was not only expected—it was virtually guaranteed.

On August 4, 1964, Captain Herrick radioed Washington that both destroyers were under North Vietnamese attack. The two vessels fired in every direction and gyrated wildly to avoid incoming torpedoes. Soon, however, Herrick wired his superiors that the "entire action leaves many doubts." Interviews with every crew member on both ships revealed that not a single sailor had actually seen or heard North Vietnamese gunfire. The strong possibility exists that an inexperienced radio operator aboard the *Maddox* had mistaken "blips" on his radar screen for enemy boats. Johnson was later reported as saying that he wasn't sure what actually had happened in the Gulf of Tonkin. "For all I know," said the President, "our navy was shooting at whales out there."

At the time, Washington sincerely believed that American warships were under attack. Although reports of the incident were fuzzy, Johnson vowed that this time he would act and ask for congressional backing for his policies. Nevertheless, to secure that backing he deliberately misled Congress and the American people. He revealed nothing about the raids on the North Vietnamese coastal stations, indicating instead that the *Maddox* had simply been engaged in a routine patrol in international waters.

The Gulf of Tonkin Resolution The next day, American warplanes roared into action, attacking North Vietnamese coastal bases as well as a nearby oil refinery. As many as 25 North Vietnamese vessels were hit, while two American planes were lost. The pilot of one plane, Lieutenant **Everett Alvarez, Jr.**, of San Jose, California, was captured. Imprisoned for more than eight years, he was the first of nearly 600 American airmen to be downed by the North Vietnamese during the Vietnam War.

Meanwhile, a broadened version of the previously prepared resolution—giving Johnson the authority to widen the war—was offered in Congress. The **Gulf of Tonkin Resolution** empowered the President to take "all necessary measures to repel any armed attack against the forces of the United States and to prevent further aggression." As Johnson later said, the resolution was "like grandma's nightshirt—it covered everything."

The nation stood behind the President in this time of crisis, and so did Congress. The vote approving the resolution was overwhelming—416-0 in the House and 88-2 in the Senate. The two opposing senators, viewed at the time as antipatriotic cranks, were **Ernest Gruening** of Alaska and **Wayne Morse** of Oregon. In words that gained him great notoriety, Morse explained: "I believe that history will record we have made a great mistake.... We are in effect giving the President war-making powers in the absence of a declaration of war."[2]

For the moment, however, Johnson had what he wanted. He had the legal authority, granted by Congress, to wage war against

---

[2] Morse was vindicated in 1970, when Congress repealed the resolution.

THE VIETNAM WAR

what he called a "raggedy-ass little fourth-rate country." He was not eager to go to war and had, in fact, restricted air raids against North Vietnam to just the one day. But he and his aides were determined. They were now prepared, furthermore, to take from the South Vietnamese government complete management of the war against the Communists.

SECTION 2 REVIEW

1. **Vocabulary to Know** covert, Gulf of Tonkin, Gulf of Tonkin Resolution

2. **People to Identify** Everett Alvarez, Jr., Ernest Gruening, Wayne Morse

3. In what ways was the United States involved in covert activity in Vietnam in 1964?

4. What was the *Maddox* doing in the Gulf of Tonkin?

5. What event led to passage of the Gulf of Tonkin Resolution?

6. **Critical Thinking** What advantages would the Gulf of Tonkin Resolution offer Johnson in the months and years to come?

3 THE UNITED STATES BECOMES FULLY INVOLVED IN THE VIETNAM WAR

In the months immediately following passage of the Gulf of Tonkin Resolution, the South Vietnamese government was in a state of near anarchy. Coups and counter-coups, demonstrations and protest rallies, fighting between Catholics and Buddhists—all these paralyzed the government. At one point Ambassador Taylor, driven to despair, lectured a group of military officers. "Do all of you understand English?" he began abruptly, abandoning the French normally used by diplomats. Then he scolded them like schoolboys, saying that "you have made a real mess. We cannot carry you forever if you do things like this." But, as always, the South Vietnamese knew that the Americans, committed to winning the war against the Communists, would not leave.

Policy Debate In Washington, American policy-makers debated what to do next. On one side there were those like **William**

THE FIGHTING INTENSIFIES (1963–1967)

Bundy, Assistant Secretary of State for Far Eastern Affairs, who called for added pressure on North Vietnam. Bundy backed the regular bombing of North Vietnamese bridges, railroads, and oil storage facilities as well as the mining of Haiphong harbor (the gateway for much of the Communists' outside support). The Joint Chiefs of Staff agreed, saying that such bombing would relieve the pressure on the Saigon government, giving it time to gain strength. Even the Joint Chiefs, however, would not go so far as Walt Rostow (page 40), who urged that American troops be sent to Vietnam immediately.

On the other side there were those like Ambassador Taylor, who believed there should be no Americans involved in a land war in Asia. Taylor feared that the bombing of North Vietnam would lead to increased Vietcong attacks in the South and that the inevitable result would be direct American combat intervention. With others, Taylor believed that North Vietnam, for the most part a rural society with a deeply motivated population, could not be blasted "back to the Stone Age," as Curtis LeMay was urging.

One lonely voice, that of Under Secretary of State **George Ball,** went further than anyone else in calling for a political solution as a means of avoiding further American involvement. "Once we are on the tiger's back," Ball wrote, "we cannot be sure of picking the place to dismount." Such a view shocked other administration figures, who had never questioned America's commitment to South Vietnam.

Delaying Intervention During these months, Lyndon Johnson still hoped to delay or avoid direct American intervention. George Ball wrote at this time that he found the President "the most reluctant to expand America's involvement." Worrying about the rise in battlefield activity, however, Johnson knew that he would eventually have to act.

One acknowledgment of the fighting came in a special White House ceremony in December when President Johnson awarded the first Medal of Honor of the Vietnam War to Captain **Roger Donlon.** In July, 1964, Donlon and his twelve-man detachment of Green Berets had valiantly defended the Nam Dong Special Forces camp, fifteen miles from Laos. Like nearly all the Americans, Donlon was wounded in the attack, but he successfully held out against an estimated 900 Vietcong guerrillas.

Because of Johnson's delays, the Communists believed he would not intervene in strength. Beginning in December, 1964, they attacked government outposts and villages throughout South Vietnam. The largest attack was against a Catholic village, Binh Gia, just forty miles from Saigon. After occupying the village for eight hours, they ambushed seven battalions of South Vietnam's best troops who had been sent into battle.

Not long after, on Christmas Eve, a bomb was exploded in a Saigon hotel which was used by American officers. Two Americans were killed and 58 injured. Every senior American official in Vietnam, including Ambassador Taylor, now urged Johnson to retaliate by bombing North Vietnam. Again, the President hesitated, fearful of intensifying the war.

The Attack on Pleiku In February, 1965, two important visitors traveled to Vietnam. One was Soviet Prime Minister Aleksei Kosygin, who met with North Vietnamese leaders. Kosygin was at the time advancing a policy of "peaceful coexistence" with the United States. He was prepared to offer the North more aid on the condition that a compromise to the Vietnamese conflict be pursued. Ho Chi Minh was not pleased by what Kosygin had to say.

McGeorge Bundy, head of the National Security Council, was at the same time in Saigon, assessing the situation. While there, he received news of a Vietcong attack on an American base near **Pleiku,** in the central highlands. Pleiku was the site of a South Vietnamese army headquarters from which patrols were sent to attack Communist infiltration routes from the North. Just outside the town was an airstrip and a fortified camp where a detachment of Green Berets were billeted.

On the night of February 6, the Vietcong struck Pleiku in a surprise attack. Mortar shells rained on the American barracks, while guerrillas raced to the airstrip, blowing up parked helicopters and planes. Several Americans died in their bunks. By the time the attack was over, seven Americans had been killed and more than a hundred were wounded. Ten aircraft were destroyed as well.

The Bombing of North Vietnam Begins Upon hearing the news from Pleiku, Bundy cabled Johnson that the United States absolutely had to act. Anything less than the continuous bombing of North Vietnam, he said, would convince the Communists "that we do not have the will ... to take the necessary action and stay the course." Johnson agreed, telling his security advisers, "I've had enough of this." Using frontier images, he angrily said, "We have kept our guns over the mantel and our shells in the cupboard for a long time, and what is the result? They are killing our men while they sleep at night."

Within hours, Operation Flaming Dart was under way, as American planes struck targets north of the seventeenth parallel.

THE FIGHTING INTENSIFIES (1963-1967)

Because of bad weather, the raids did little damage to the North Vietnamese. In fact, they had an unanticipated benefit. Prime Minister Kosygin, still in Hanoi, announced that the Soviet Union would increase its aid to North Vietnam with no strings attached. Until then, the North Vietnamese had depended almost entirely on assistance from China.

The "Credibility Gap" Although advised by his aides and the Joint Chiefs to go to the American people and lay out the facts about the difficult situation facing the United States in Vietnam, Johnson refused. Already, critics were accusing him of not being fully honest, and there was talk of a **"credibility gap"**—the difference between what Johnson said and what was true. During these days, while holding policy meetings on Vietnam, the President told the press, "I know of no far-reaching strategy that is being suggested."

Johnson had his reasons for being less than candid. He did not want to alarm the public; nor did he want to risk Soviet or Chinese intervention by making warlike statements. The result, however, was that the country was sinking deeper into war without many people knowing about it.

The Air War Few Americans knew much about Rolling Thunder, the next in the series of bombing programs against North Vietnam. These raids, which would go on for the following three years, grew bigger and bigger. Among the aircraft that hit North Vietnam were the mighty B-52's, which were capable of carrying a conventional bomb load of 60,000 pounds. They also were armed with **napalm** (a jelly-like substance which adheres while it burns) and **cluster bombs** (explosives containing hundreds of pellets which burst out at high velocity to rip deep into the body of anyone within range).

The American reliance on airpower was based on the theory, held by many administration figures, that bombing would destroy the enemy's will to fight. Still, this theory had met with only limited success in World War II and the Korean War. The special situation of Vietnam added further problems. For one thing, Johnson resisted the Joint Chiefs' proposal for total war, fearing that a full-scale attack on North Vietnam might lead to Chinese intervention. The President maintained tight personal control over the bombings and even boasted at one point, "they can't even bomb an outhouse without my approval." Only gradually, as each phase of the bombing failed to bring the North Vietnamese to the peace table, did Johnson expand the list of targets and the number of strikes. At the start, however, railroads leading from China to

Hanoi were off target so as not to provoke the Chinese, while extreme care was taken in bombing Haiphong because Soviet supply ships were frequently anchored there. Hanoi was spared too, the theory being that the threat of its destruction could be held as a major bargaining chip. Throughout the war, finally, targets were also chosen that would not endanger the civilian population.[3]

North Vietnam learned to adapt to the bombing raids. City dwellers were evacuated to the countryside, industries were scattered and sometimes even moved to caves and tunnels, and thousands of people were mobilized to keep transportation routes open. For instance, piles of gravel were kept alongside all major highways, so that craters could be filled within hours after the bombs fell. White markers were placed along roads so that truck drivers could travel at night, without headlights.

For all the losses that the air raids inflicted—and they were substantial—the North Vietnamese were able to replace lost military equipment, vehicles, and raw materials with increased aid from China and the Soviet Union. Soviet assistance was especially important, for after 1965 the North Vietnamese received surface-to-air missiles and fighter planes, which stiffened the nation's air defenses.

Finally, there was another factor that limited the effectiveness of the air raids. Each year the long monsoon season, from September to May, brought heavy rains and dense fog to Indochina. As a result, the bad weather made it extremely difficult for pilots to hit their assigned targets.

By the end of the Vietnam War, the United States had dropped three times more bombs on North Vietnam, an area the size of Texas, than it had on all of Europe, Asia, and Africa during World War II. Yet the bombing did not achieve its goals. It never stopped the movement of troops and supplies south. Nor did it force the Communists to negotiate. Even worse, it cost the United States many billions of dollars to pay for the air war. The cost of the 950 aircraft lost between 1965 and 1968, for example, was $6 billion. Finally, captured American pilots gave Hanoi a bargaining chip that it would later use to full advantage.[4]

The First Combat Troops With American planes now regularly flying missions, General Westmoreland worried that the main

---

[3]. More care was taken in avoiding civilian targets in the North, in fact, than in the South.
[4]. The bombing of the South continued throughout the war, even during the many halts in the air strikes against the North. In spite of the widespread devastation, the air war was not able to end Communist support in the South.

American airfield in South Vietnam, at **Danang,** might be attacked by guerrillas in the area. He asked Johnson to send two Marine battalions to protect the base. Ambassador Taylor strongly objected to the request, again voicing his concerns that American combat troops would be no more effective than the French. "The white-faced soldier," he advised Washington, "armed, equipped, and trained as he is, is not a suitable guerrilla fighter for Asian forests and jungles." But Johnson quickly approved Westmoreland's request.

On March 8, 1965, the first American combat troops splashed ashore on the Asian mainland since the end of the Korean War. In a carefully staged arrival, they were greeted at Danang not by hostile gunfire but by young Vietnamese women, smiling and handing out flowers.

The decision to commit troops to Vietnam had been made without fully notifying the American people or Congress. Johnson suggested that the troops were there only for defensive purposes and as a response to the Pleiku attack, rather than as a measure to prevent the collapse of South Vietnam. He even hinted that they would soon be withdrawn. Not until June, when the news was released *by accident* in a press release, did the administration reveal that American troops were authorized to undertake offensive operations.

Johnson ignored the advice of the Joint Chiefs and of Secretary McNamara to put the nation on a war footing and to explain to the public the American role in Vietnam.[5] A major corner had been turned, and in the months and years that followed, the demand for more troops would be heard with frequency.

The request for additional troops came all too soon. Westmoreland wanted more manpower, and on April 1, 1965, he got two Marine battalions plus 20,000 **logistical troops** (that is, behind-the-scene troops who handle supplies). The marines were eager to see action. "This is a grunt battalion," one rifleman said, "not a bunch of gate guards." A Marine commander agreed, saying that his men were going to "start killing the Vietcong instead of just sitting on their ditty box." Westmoreland also wanted the troops out patrolling the countryside, not merely defending installations along the coast.

[5.] Administration spokesmen were always vague in their public pronouncements about the American role in Vietnam. Sometimes they mentioned the need to contain communism; sometimes China was stressed; sometimes it was wars of liberation that were being confronted.

VIETNAM FACT

*The **M16 rifle**, a new automatic weapon, was introduced by the United States military in 1965. It quickly became the subject of controversy. The M16 was light and easy to handle, and it could fire 700 rounds of .22 caliber bullets a minute. Many troops complained bitterly about the weapon, however, claiming that it had a disturbing tendency to jam after firing several rounds. In several instances soldiers were killed in battle while trying to fix their rifles. In 1967, during a congressional investigation of charges that the M16 was unfit for combat in Vietnam, it was learned that the rifle was delicate and required careful cleaning and maintenance. Troops were instructed in how to care for the M16, and its design was slightly changed. Despite the early controversy, the M16 continues to be used by all the United States military services today.*

Instability in Saigon One reason the American command in Vietnam was eager to take direction of the war against the Communists was the instability of the Saigon government. Ever since the overthrow of Diem, the make-up of that government was constantly changing. In August, 1964, following the Tonkin Gulf affair, General Khanh had tried to assume dictatorial powers. Thousands of protestors had taken to the streets, forcing Khanh to resign in humiliation. Soon a group of young officers took over, allowing Khanh to go into exile as an ambassador-at-large to the United States and Europe. Now, in June, 1965, there was another shake-up. General **Nguyen Van Thieu** was made chief of state while Air Vice Marshal **Nguyen Cao Ky** became prime minister.

The situation in Saigon, as well as increasing Vietcong dominance in the countryside, prompted Westmoreland to call for still more American troops. He wanted 180,000 men immediately, and another 100,000 in 1966. "We are in for the long pull," he privately told the President. "I see no likelihood of achieving a quick, favorable end to the war." On July 28, 1965, in a midday television speech when the viewing audience is small, Johnson announced that he had agreed to Westmoreland's request.

Escalation By the start of 1966, there were nearly 200,000 American soldiers in Vietnam. The Communists, however, were

THE FIGHTING INTENSIFIES (1963-1967)

beefing up their forces too, bringing troops south at twice the rate of the United States. The word **escalation** began to be used to describe the situation. That is, one side would raise the stakes and widen the war, and the other side would respond in kind.

The Communists needed the additional support, because of the presence of so many newly arrived Americans. After securing the area around Danang, American units had crushed three North Vietnamese regiments in the Ia Drang valley, near Pleiku. In the Ia Drang operation, B-52's had proved especially effective in providing air support to the men on the ground. Three hundred Americans died in the battle, but nearly two thousand North Vietnamese had been killed. Westmoreland was convinced that the favorable **"kill ratio"** would ensure eventual success.

A "Peace Offensive" Throughout 1965, as the escalation continued, some administration figures had begun having second thoughts about American policy. Robert McNamara, in particular, was shaken by the failure to halt the movement of North Vietnamese troops south along the Ho Chi Minh Trail. He doubted, furthermore, that even 600,000 Americans could guarantee victory in Vietnam. He was aware too of the first stirrings of antiwar protests at home.

McNamara proposed that the air strikes against the North be halted before more Americans were sent to Vietnam. He hoped this gesture would give the Communists a face-saving chance to agree to a diplomatic settlement of the conflict. Johnson announced this, the first of many bombing halts, on Christmas morning. During the 37 days that the bombing was called off, a public relations campaign was carried out, trying to convince the North Vietnamese of the administration's sincerity. The "peace offensive" went nowhere. Set back on the battlefield in the South, the Communists had no intention of making concessions at the bargaining table.

The Fulbright Hearings A few days after the bombing of the North resumed, the Senate Foreign Relations Committee, chaired by **J. William Fulbright,** began nationally televised hearings. Senator Fulbright, an eloquent scholar from Arkansas and until then a Johnson loyalist, had grown troubled by the handling of the Vietnam conflict. Fulbright was on his way to becoming one of Johnson's most irritating critics, and later that spring, in a memorable phrase, would accuse the administration of an "arrogance of power."

The hearings, meanwhile, provided Americans with an opportunity to consider the nation's role in Vietnam. The questioning of administration officials was polite, and little new was learned. But at a time when Johnson was still playing down the impact the war was having on the nation,[6] television was focusing the public's attention on Vietnam in an important way.

Private Doubts Publicly the administration preached optimism, but as 1966 turned into 1967, private doubts continued to grow. McNamara, especially, had come to the conclusion that the bombing campaign was having no direct effect on North Vietnam's military activities. Desperately he cast about for a way out, even suggesting that the Vietcong be invited to share political power in the South.

Johnson, meanwhile, stopped off in Vietnam during an Asian tour. Flying to the American base at Camranh Bay, he urged a crowd of awed GI's to "nail the coonskin to the wall." Johnson too was torn, however, and he continued to avoid making difficult decisions. Escalation was no guarantee of victory, he recognized, and he feared that if too many Americans poured into Vietnam, Ho Chi Minh would simply call in the Chinese. Johnson remembered all too well that the Korean conflict had nearly ended in disaster when China had entered the war. He continued to give the generals most of what they wanted—new targets in North Vietnam, more American troops in South Vietnam—but he was not happy about it.

The Departure of McNamara In the early 1960's, the Vietnam conflict had been called "McNamara's War," and the Secretary of Defense had not objected. But by 1967 Robert McNamara's doubts had reached the point where Johnson viewed him as disloyal.

In mid-year, the pro-military Preparedness Subcommittee of the Senate Armed Services Committee held closed hearings to investigate why "unskilled civilian amateurs" were being allowed to hinder the efforts of "professional military experts." The senators on the subcommittee were particularly eager to hear from McNamara—presumably one of those "unskilled civilian amateurs." What McNamara had to say did not please them. The bombing of the North, he stated bluntly, had failed. Enemy operations in the South, he went on, would not be affected by the bombing unless the United States were ready to embark on a policy of **genocide**—the killing of all the inhabitants of North Vietnam.

These comments, and others, convinced Johnson that Mc-

[6.] Not until 1967, for instance, would the President ask Congress for a tax increase to pay for the enormous costs of the war.

THE FIGHTING INTENSIFIES (1963-1967)

Namara had to go. The President was also concerned about McNamara's friendship with Robert Kennedy. Elected in 1964 as a senator from New York, Kennedy had recently emerged as a leading critic of the war. A position was found for McNamara as president of the World Bank, and he was replaced as Secretary of Defense in February, 1968, by **Clark Clifford,** a Washington lawyer and an old friend of Johnson's.

Deadlock By the end of 1967 there were nearly 500,000 American troops in Vietnam, 100,000 more than the year before. Approximately 9,000 Americans had been killed in that year, and yet there was no end in sight. The war, for all purposes, was deadlocked.

With an election year fast approaching, and with public impatience of his handling of the war on the rise, Johnson relied on familiar tactics. In his appearances and speeches he promoted optimism and confidence. He also brought Westmoreland home to tour the nation and paint a rosy picture. "The enemy's hopes are bankrupt," Westmoreland proclaimed in Washington. "The ranks of the Vietcong are thinning steadily." To a magazine reporter, he boasted, "I hope they try something, because we are looking for a fight." He would soon get more than he or the American people had bargained for.

SECTION 3 REVIEW

1. **Vocabulary to Know** Pleiku, "credibility gap," napalm, cluster bomb, Danang, logistical troops, escalation, "kill ratio," genocide

2. **People to Identify** William Bundy, George Ball, McGeorge Bundy, Roger Donlon, Nguyen Van Thieu, Nguyen Cao Ky, J. William Fulbright, Clark Clifford

3. Why was the Communist attack on Pleiku a significant event?

4. For what reasons was Johnson less than candid about the deepening American role in Vietnam?

5. When and where did the first American combat troops arrive in Vietnam?

6. What doubts did Robert McNamara have about America's Vietnam policies?

7. **Critical Thinking** Of what symbolic importance was McNamara's departure from the administration?

CHAPTER 3 REVIEW

Vocabulary and People

Everett Alvarez, Jr.
George Ball
McGeorge Bundy
William Bundy
Clark Clifford
cluster bomb
covert
"credibility gap"
Danang
Roger Donlon
escalation
J. William Fulbright
genocide

Barry Goldwater
Ernest Gruening
Gulf of Tonkin
Gulf of Tonkin Resolution
Nguyen Khanh
"kill ratio"
Nguyen Cao Ky
logistical troops
Wayne Morse
napalm
Pleiku
Nguyen Van Thieu
William Westmoreland

Identification

On a separate sheet of paper, match the following people with the numbered phrase that describes them: *Clark Clifford, J. William Fulbright, Robert McNamara, Wayne Morse, William Westmoreland.*

1. _____ led opposition to the Gulf of Tonkin Resolution.

2. The American military commander in Vietnam, _____ sought an active role for his troops.

3. Upon the departure of Robert McNamara, _____ became Secretary of Defense.

4. Lyndon Johnson defeated _____ in a landslide victory in 1964.

5. Senate hearings to investigate American involvement in Vietnam were headed by _____.

Reviewing the Main Ideas

1. What evidence was there of government instability in South Vietnam during the mid-1960's?

THE FIGHTING INTENSIFIES (1963-1967)

2. (a) Why was passage of the Gulf of Tonkin Resolution such a key event? (b) How would you describe the circumstances of its passage?

3. In what ways was the American bombing of North Vietnam a failure?

4. What were the dangers for Johnson in allowing a "credibility gap" to develop?

5. What was the situation in Vietnam by the end of 1967?

Critical Thinking

In accepting the Republican presidential nomination in 1964, Barry Goldwater had this to say about Vietnam. Read his comments and then answer the questions that follow:

> Now, we Americans understand freedom, we have earned it; we have lived for it, and we have died for it. This nation and its people are freedom's models in a searching world. We can be freedom's missionaries in a doubting world....
>
> Yesterday it was Korea; tonight it is Vietnam. Make no bones of this. Don't try to sweep this under the rug. We are at war in Vietnam. And yet the President, who is the commander in chief of our forces, refuses to say, refuses to say, mind you, whether or not the objective over there is victory, and his Secretary of Defense continues to mislead and misinform the American people.

1. What, according to Goldwater, does Johnson refuse to say?

2. Goldwater says that Americans are "freedom's missionaries." What does that suggest about the type of foreign policy he favored?

3. What kind of policy do you think Goldwater would have followed in Vietnam? Explain your answer.

President Lyndon B. Johnson discusses Vietnam policy at a White House meeting.

CHAPTER FOUR

A DIFFERENT WAR

IN AUGUST, 1965, AMERICANS WATCHING THE evening news on CBS were startled by what they saw. Television cameras had followed a company of marines into a complex of villages known as Cam Ne, where as many as 100 enemy soldiers were thought to be entrenched. A Vietminh stronghold during the war against the French, Cam Ne had remained in Communist hands, and it clearly was dangerous territory.

As the marines approached Cam Ne, they were fired upon by snipers from behind civilian huts. It was impossible to tell who was doing the shooting, however, as no enemy troops were actually seen. In such areas, civilians and guerrillas all looked alike—and, in many cases, they were one and the same. Still, whoever was firing had wounded four marines, and the Americans responded by setting fire to the village. Over 150 huts were burned as the cameras rolled, and the American public was suddenly confronted with a new kind of war—one where marines lit dwellings with cigarette lighters, burning them to the ground, while elderly peasants wailed in the background.

It was a new kind of war, both for the troops in the field as well as for the American public. A Marine officer described best the difficult reality of Vietnam and what made the war there so frustrating: "For the first time we're faced with a war that is 80 percent political and 20 percent conventional military. But when a man in the line is getting shot at, he is prone to consider the war to be 100 percent military."

In this chapter you will read how the American military adapted to this new warfare. You will read too how the American public began to lose patience with it. As you read, look for answers to the following questions:

1. How was the Vietnam War different from other wars?
2. Why did the Vietnam War threaten to divide the United States?

1 THE VIETNAM WAR IS DIFFERENT FROM OTHER WARS

The year 1965 saw the beginning of the big American build-up in Vietnam. Soon, troops were exposed to that country's heat and rains, they were sniped at and booby trapped by unseen guerrillas, and they discovered that it was almost impossible to find anyone to stand and fight.

Westmoreland's Strategy From the time William Westmoreland took command of American operations in Vietnam in June, 1964, it was apparent that the Johnson administration had found an efficient, disciplined, organization man. Within weeks of arriving in Saigon, he developed strategies that he believed would end in victory.

The first part of Westmoreland's plan was called **search and destroy.** American troops would carry out operations in which they were to "find, fix in place, fight, and destroy" enemy forces. Once an area had been "cleared" of guerrillas, South Vietnamese forces would be assigned the task of "securing" the countryside. They would also provide permanent defense to prevent the enemy from returning.

Westmoreland's strategy called for large numbers of American troops, more than he was ever able to persuade Washington to send. It was also based on the assumption that superior American firepower would make the decisive difference.

In its major military efforts—the Civil War, World War I, World War II—the United States had learned the value of superior firepower. The arms and ammunition that northern industry had provided in abundance led to the defeat of the Confederacy; the same thing had happened to Germany in both world wars. In Vietnam too, even if there were manpower shortages, the overwhelming superiority in arms, it was felt, would defeat the Communists.

Small units, then, were sent out on patrol, almost as bait, hoping to make contact with the elusive enemy so that the firepower could be called in. The firepower available to the American ground troops was awesome indeed: artillery from nearby bases, from offshore vessels, from helicopter gunships, and from jets straffing and bombing. But there were problems with this approach. The massive bombing brought added harm to the precarious South Vietnamese economy, virtually destroying its agriculture and sending huge numbers of civilians to the cities in search of safety. The government in Saigon had never been popular, and now the people had even more reason to dislike it. One American official later said of the bombing, "It was as if we were trying to build a house with a bulldozer and wrecking crane."

For all the time and effort that was spent on the "search-and-destroy" missions, moreover, almost never did enemy troops fire and reveal their positions. One study concluded that American patrols during all of 1967-1968 made contact with the enemy in less than 1 percent of the cases. When the patrols of ARVN troops were included, the percentage fell to one-tenth of 1 percent. On those rare occasions when contact was made, moreover, it was often with a handful of snipers who were covering the retreat of the main force. In more than half of all cases, the fights were too small or over too quickly to call in firepower.

The Enclave Theory Not all American military leaders approved of Westmoreland's strategy. In the early years of the war, debate went on between those favoring the more aggressive search-and-destroy approach and those advancing the so-called **enclave theory.** Under the enclave theory, the chief emphasis was placed on the enclave, or area, that had been occupied. The marines, in particular, saw their responsibility as one of providing absolute security for the population under their control. They were, in short, more concerned with people than with occupying large stretches of territory.

Westmoreland believed in the need of attacking the enemy forces, to keep them off balance. To do this, however, he too often had to remove his troops from the population centers along the coast to have them pursue the enemy in the mountains. After the war, Lieutenant General Victor Krulak, a top Marine commander, said bluntly, "Every man we put into hunting for the NVA was wasted." But Westmoreland was commander of all the

American forces in Vietnam, and eventually his methods were those that were followed.

VIETNAM FACT

The United States was not the only nation to send troops to South Vietnam. Small numbers of soldiers from the Philippines and Thailand fought in Vietnam, as did more than 8,000 Australians and 1,000 New Zealanders. The largest troop contribution came from South Korea. Nearly 50,000 South Koreans, paid for by the United States, served in South Vietnam. The Vietcong so feared the tough South Koreans that they ordered contact with them "to be avoided at all costs unless a victory is 100 percent certain."

The Battle of Chu Lai An early battle demonstrated the difficulties of any strategy the Americans might follow. In August 1965, the marines had recently arrived in the coastal Cam Ne area. The Vietcong, nicknamed **"Charlie"** by the newly arrived Americans, were seeking to win an early psychological victory. They made plans to surprise an isolated Marine base at Chu Lai, but a deserter tipped off the Americans, who quickly went on the attack.

Heavy fighting spread across the countryside. At one point, when the Vietcong tried to ambush a relief column, air support proved decisive. An American general later said that bombs were dropped "within 200 feet of our pinned down troops and was a very important factor in our winning the battle. I have never seen a finer example of *close* air support."

Due in large part to the overwhelming American advantage in firepower—even two navy ships, lying just off the coast, provided fire support—the battle ended in a Vietcong defeat. The marines were justifiably proud that in their first major battle in Vietnam —known as the **Battle of Chu Lai**—they had emerged victorious. But the Communists had learned from the battle too. In the future they would rarely choose to stand and fight the Americans; instead, they would rely on small-scale guerrilla tactics.

Attrition Before long the word **attrition** was being used to describe Westmoreland's battle plan. Westmoreland and many others assumed that enemy troops would suffer so many casualties that they could no longer go on fighting. "We'll just go on bleeding them," Westmoreland said, "until Hanoi wakes up to the fact that they have bled their country to the point of national disaster for generations."

At what point, however, would attrition succeed? As time went on and as Communist casualties mounted, enemy strength actually increased. Every year some 300,000 North Vietnamese reached draft age, and Westmoreland estimated that 100,000 of them were able to move south, where they joined the 50,000 guerrillas recruited annually in South Vietnam. The Communists were easily able, then, to match the American troop build-up.

Measures of Progress The Vietnam War was a different war from any other major conflict fought by the United States for the simple reason that it was a war without fronts and without battlelines. Unlike a conventional war, such as World War II or even the Korean War, the entire country was a battlefield—from the rice fields of the Meking Delta, to the deep forests and wetlands north of Saigon, to the dense jungle and rugged hills along the border with Laos and North Vietnam. There was no real way, in such a conflict, to measure how much progress was being made. Positions could be captured—often at great cost—only to be followed by their abandonment to the enemy. Even an area thought to be secure might suddenly be hit by enemy raiders.

Washington and the American public expected, however, that progress be made and that it be demonstrated. A number of measures of progress were developed, though none gave an accurate picture of what was really happening.

One way the military command measured progress was to provide regular **body counts.** After each engagement, Americans were ordered to provide an accurate count of how many enemy fighters had been killed. So long as the North Vietnamese and Vietcong were able to replace their forces, however, body counts had no significant meaning.

Another measure of progess was called **battalion days in the field,** days in which Americans were out on patrol. Since so little contact with the enemy was ever made, this statistic also lacked importance.

A third statistic was proved equally meaningless. Commanders were encouraged to present evidence of progress in guaranteeing the security of roads and railroads—their careers often depended on it—and they tended to exaggerate progress. The security of these transportation links could never be totally guaranteed, moreover, since they were subject to enemy ambush.

Guerrilla Warfare When Americans first started arriving in Vietnam in large numbers, they encountered all the frustrations of guerrilla warfare. The Americans outnumbered their adversaries and they had superior arms and supplies. The Communists, however, had distinct advantages too. For one thing, the swamps and jungles of Vietnam offered them protection. Sanctuaries across the border in Cambodia and Laos were invaluable too. Finally, the Communists could usually count on the support of the local population. At times that support was gained through terrorist methods. But it was often genuine, particularly in the early 1960's. "The soldiers came from the people," recalled one Communist organizer. "They were the children of the villages. They were the people's soldiers."

A chief goal of the guerrilla fighters was to avoid combat with superior forces. On those rare occasions when they did engage in battle, they made sure the combat was carried out on their terms. Before they attacked a target, they would carefully rehearse their battle plan, sometimes for weeks in advance.

A main part of the Communists' strategy was the ambush. First a detachment would pin down an enemy unit, sometimes engaging in hand-to-hand combat.[1] Then the main force, which had been held back, would ambush advancing reinforcements. Indeed, attacks were often staged for the sole purpose of luring relief columns into a trap.

Booby Traps These attacks, however, were far from common. The primary goal of the guerrillas was to wear down the Americans, to frustrate them and damage their **morale** (their spirit or enthusiasm) through sneak attacks and through booby traps.

The various booby traps of the guerrilla fighters posed constant hazards to American infantrymen. There were animal snares which, when tripped, catapulted and held their prey upside down, high above the ground. There were camouflaged holes filled with razor-sharp *punji* stakes, sometimes poisoned, that could pierce a soldier's feet, legs, and stomach if he stumbled into one. As the war went on, the guerrillas increasingly made use of carefully hidden land mines, or of grenades triggered by concealed trip wires. GI's could go for weeks without making contact with the enemy—in fact, most never did—but there was always the possibility of sudden danger.

American Innovations Americans did their best to adapt to guerrilla warfare. New techniques were effectively introduced.

---

[1] The Communists learned to get as close as possible to American positions so that air attacks could not be called in, out of fear of hitting the GI's.

One, the "flare-and-strike" technique, used flares dropped from a plane to permit night operations. There were the highly successful "Eagle Fights" as well, in which helicopters circled above contested terrain, ready to swoop down on any groups fleeing advancing American or ARVN forces.

Among the ingenious gadgets and inventions were electrified barbed wire, **defoliant** chemicals which destroyed the enemy's ground cover, and electronic sensors. Taking a page from the guerrillas, the Americans also introduced the *kpung,* a poisonous nettle causing excruciating pain and used as a barrier around positions threatened by Communist attack.

Yet all these innovations were of little value if the *other* war—the war to win the backing of the Vietnamese people—could not be won. Some called this effort the war for the **hearts and minds** of the people; others called it **pacification.** Whatever its name, it was important because the loyalty of the people was the most important tool of the government in the fight against the Communists.

Over the years ambitious social and economic programs were advanced as a means of achieving pacification. For the most part, however, the American high command was convinced that the path to victory was through military success. They had little patience with pacification.

Guns and Butter The American leadership also assumed that they could win the war without asking the American people to make sacrifices. In 1965, as the war was beginning to heat up, President Johnson was reluctant to call a halt to his ambitious Great Society programs. Congress had passed fewer than half the bills he had submitted, and he feared that the Great Society would be doomed if the public's attention were too strongly focused on the Vietnam War. He wanted both—to carry on the effort in Vietnam and to pass the Great Society legislation—but he wanted them without having to raise taxes. He wanted **guns and butter,** and for a time it looked as if he would get them.

Supplying the Troops Certainly the effort to supply the military with every conceivable need was going ahead full steam by 1965. The supplies sent to South Vietnam would end by surpassing the World War II figures, and the effort was in itself an amazing achievement.

The following random statistics from 1965 indicate the sheer volume of goods supplied to the troops:

• the Oscar Mayer plant in Madison, Wisconsin, turned out 2.6 million canned hams for shipment to the troops.

- Chicago's Borg-Warner Company began sending more than 700,000 steel helmets to the army, which had bought no new helmets since 1958.
- in Huntsville, Alabama, the Safety First Shoe Company worked on an order of 253,907 pairs of nylon-topped jungle boots.
- Rossi & Sons of Vineland, New Jersey, shipped out its first order for 100,000 tropical raincoats.
- Kaiser Jeep received a $58 million order for jeeps.
- the army placed a $258 million order for some 1,600 helicopters.

The incredible logistical effort[2] was aimed at providing the soldiers with all that was comfortable and familiar during their time in Vietnam.[3] For instance, over 90 percent of their meals were served hot. Forty ice cream plants and three dairies were set up in Vietnam. Post Exchanges (PX's) offered every conceivable item —from televisions to cameras, panty hose to diamonds, sports clothes to deodorants. In all, the Americans who fought in Vietnam were the best fed, best clothed, and best equipped of any force ever sent to war.

More than food and equipment, of course, was sent to Vietnam. Army engineers and contractors worked around the clock, carving out roads, dredging rivers, building fuel depots and warehouses. Six deep-draft harbors were built, and so were scores of helicopter pads and airbases. (So heavy was the air traffic that South Vietnam's airports became the busiest in the world.) Communications systems were installed, linking remote parts of the country and connecting South Vietnam with the rest of the world. Soon, President Johnson could call Saigon direct within a matter of seconds.

To entertain the troops and boost morale, numerous celebrities performed in Vietnam. Among the favorites was comedienne Martha Raye, who traveled to Vietnam time after time, once staying for five months. Under fire on several occasions, she was admired for her courage and, of course, for her humor. Christmas visits by Bob Hope, often broadcast to stateside audiences, were annual events. Among other entertainers who gave of their time and talent were actors Charlton Heston, John Wayne, and Raymond Burr; actresses Jill St. John, Raquel Welch, Ann-

---

[2.] Most American troops in Vietnam—at least 80 percent—were involved in the logistical effort. Their tours of duty, in the relative security of rear bases, was quite different from that of the grunts involved in battlefield combat.

[3.] For reasons of morale, Westmoreland had limited each soldier's tour in Vietnam to 365 days.

Margret, Lana Turner, and Julie Andrews; comics Phyllis Diller, Redd Foxx, and Edgar Bergen; and singers Vic Damone, Nancy Sinatra, and Eddie Fisher. Other noted visitors included columnist Ann Landers, novelist John Steinbeck, Coach Woody Hayes of Ohio State University, and evangelist Billy Graham.

VIETNAM FACT

During the big American build-up in Vietnam, **Camranh,** *the site of one of the finest natural harbors in the world, was a major hub of activity. The six piers that were built at Camranh could off-load 4,000 tons of cargo a day, second only to Saigon. The navy's major communications center in South Vietnam was located there, as was the third busiest air force base in the country. In addition, Camranh was equipped with a laundry, a dairy, a 2,000-bed hospital, and housing for the more than 20,000 enlisted troops who were stationed there. The immense complex, built at a cost of more than $2 billion, is now largely deserted. What remains serves as a port of call for the Soviet navy.*

Questions Remain By 1967, a million tons of supplies a month was pouring into Vietnam. For every American in the country, in other words, an average of 100 pounds a day was being unloaded. Still, the same questions went unanswered. What good were all these supplies without the support of the South Vietnamese people? Where was the enemy? *Who* was the enemy?

One American general thought he had an answer for the last question. To tell the enemy from innocent peasants, he proposed the following: "It occurred to me that perhaps we would be able to identify the guerrilla—a farmer by day and a fighter by night—by the dark circles under his eyes." It would soon be suggested that innocent farmers might stay up late on occasion too.

As the war went on, Americans began to rely more and more on military might. At one point an officer explained, after bombing a South Vietnamese provincial capital, that "we had to destroy the town in order to save it." The explanation became a symbol of the frustration Americans encountered in Vietnam.

SECTION 1 REVIEW

1. **Vocabulary to Know** search and destroy, enclave theory, "Charlie," Battle of Chu Lai, attrition, body count, battalion days in the field, morale, defoliant, hearts and minds, pacification, guns and butter

2. What was Westmoreland's strategy to win the war?

3. What problems were there with Westmoreland's approach?

4. Why, unlike other wars, was it so hard to measure progress in Vietnam?

5. Why did President Johnson want to have both guns and butter?

6. **Critical Thinking** Why was pacification such an important part of the effort in Vietnam?

2 THE WAR THREATENS TO DIVIDE THE UNITED STATES

On November 2, 1965, a 32-year-old Quaker named Norman Morrison poured kerosene over his body, sat within view of Robert McNamara's third-floor Pentagon office, and set himself on fire. In an eerie replay of the Buddhist suicides protesting the oppression of the Diem regime, Morrison took his life to protest American policy.

The year 1965 was not a year of massive demonstrations. Still, Morrison's extreme act was a sign of the opposition that was building to the war in Vietnam.

Other Domestic Concerns Only slowly did Americans become aware of what *Newsweek* magazine was calling, in 1965, "that nagging little war in Vietnam." There was much else of more immediate concern. The civil rights movement, for example, was heating up. On March 7, 1965, state troopers violently attacked demonstrators trying to march from Selma to Montgomery, Alabama. The scenes from Selma transfixed the nation, and in the uproar that followed, the landing of the first American combat troops in Danang on the very next day received only minor attention. The majority of Americans remained, at best, ill-informed and confused about Vietnam.

The First Protests Against the War Opposition to the war was, at first, muted and confined to colleges and universities. On the day after the marines landed in Vietnam, students on a number of campuses held the first **teach-ins.** Classes were canceled as professors and students met to discuss the war. For the first time, basic questions were debated. How had the United States become involved in Vietnam? How many Americans would have to die there? What right did the United States have to be fighting there in the first place? Was the Vietnam War really only a civil war, a war of "national liberation"? As the answers to these and other questions were discussed, student protests grew.

The first notable protest against the war was organized by an organization known as **Students for a Democratic Society.** SDS, as it was called, had been founded in 1961 to work for civil rights and to end poverty. It shifted its attention to the war in Vietnam, and would become violent as the 1960's proceeded. For now, its first demonstration—attended by some 20,000 students in Washington on April 17, 1965—was entirely peaceful.

Other opponents of the administration's policy made common cause with the students. They included three main groups. First, there were Quakers and other pacifists, such as members of the Committee for a Sane Nuclear Policy (SANE) or Women's Strike for Peace, who opposed all wars as immoral. Second, there were "New Left" radicals who viewed the war as an example of the way the American ruling class was exploiting people around the world to keep capitalism in place. Finally, there were antiwar liberals who opposed the war both on practical as well as on moral grounds. This third antiwar group, which was by far the largest, viewed the war as a civil war of little concern to the United States.

Soon, those demanding an end to the fighting in Vietnam were being called **doves.** They confronted backers of the fight against communism, known as **hawks.** The hawks, while urging victory in Vietnam, were unhappy with Johnson's policy of slow, gradual troop increases, and they urged the administration to do whatever was necessary to reach victory.

The protesters were part of a long, though often lonely, heritage of resisting war in the United States. The Mexican War, never popular in the North, had been denounced by such notable Americans as Abraham Lincoln. Draft riots had scarred New York City during the Civil War. The Korean War had had its share of critics too—both conservative and liberal. But in 1965, the protesters enjoyed little public understanding. The great majority of Americans regarded them as misguided at best and as Communists at worst. *Time* magazine called the antiwar protesters "a ragtag collection of the unshaven and unscrubbed." Johnson, outraged by the early opponents to his policies, assailed them as "nervous Nellies who break ranks under the strain and turn on their leaders, their own country, and their fighting men."

The Draft As time went on, demonstrations against the Vietnam War would grow in size and number as well as in anger. Soon protesters chanted: "Hey, Hey, LBJ, How Many Kids Have You Killed Today?" More and more young men found themselves headed toward a country that most Americans could not even locate on a map, and the protests became increasingly directed against the Selective Service System, the organization responsible for drafting men into the military.

Compulsory military service, or the **draft,** had existed long before 1965, but most young men who signed up for it paid it little attention. In those days, the chances of being drafted were not great. So long as the nation stayed at peace, there were enough **exemptions** (releases or excuses) and **deferments** (postponements) available to ensure that two thirds of all those registered would reach the cut-off age of 26 without ever serving in the armed forces.

As the military effort grew in Vietnam, however, the Selective Service System began calling up larger numbers of young men. Through its 3,700 local draft boards, it sent out 13,700 induction notices in April, 1965. By December, over 40,000 notices were issued.

"Greetings," the draft notice began. And as more "greetings" were received, protests mounted. Vietnam was becoming real, and for most young men, having to fight there was not a source of pride; indeed, within a few years military service would be considered a misfortune.

With the draft symbolizing the nation's war policy, the burning of draft cards became a dramatic means of protest, even after Congress toughened the penalties against such an act. Of course, draft-card burners were in the distinct minority. Most young men found ways to avoid being drafted, rather than resist it.

Avoiding the Draft Avoidance was available to almost everyone. One way to sidestep the draft was simply to fail to register for it. For those who had already received draft notices, they could always try to join the Air Force or Navy,[4] rather than enter the Army or the Marines where the chances of going to Vietnam were greater. Enlistments in the National Guard and the reserves

---

[4.] Both the Air Force and Navy had tougher entrance requirements than the other services, however.

became popular options as well. Then too, there were those who fled to Canada or served jail sentences rather than go to Vietnam.

The many deferments and exemptions provided other ways of avoiding the draft. Exemptions for married men were ended in mid-1965, and by early 1966 college students ranking in the lower levels of their class were made eligible for military service. Still, most educational, employment, or hardship deferments remained on the books. Draft counseling centers spread, specializing in draft laws and advising young men in ways to avoid military service. Claiming "conscientious objection" to the war on moral grounds became popular. More than 50,000 men were given this classification during the war.

Failing the draft physical was the exemption that excluded the most young men. Once eligible for the draft, an individual had to pass an intelligence test and physical exam before being classified I–A ("available for military service"). Those who failed might receive a 4–F classification ("not qualified for any military service"). Many potential draftess had legitimate grounds for receiving 4–F exemptions. But to gain the highly prized exemption, some young men would artificially raise their blood pressure with drugs, fake illnesses, aggravate sports injuries, or lose or gain enough weight to exceed the military's limits for their heights.

Those Who Fought in Vietnam More than 25 percent of all potential draftees were disqualified for physical reasons. More than 30 percent used deferments or exemptions to avoid induction. Another 5 percent served in the National Guard or in the reserves. Who, then, went to Vietnam?

The typical American sent to Vietnam was poorly educated and from a low-income family. A survey found that men from disadvantaged backgrounds were about twice as likely to go to Vietnam and see combat as those who were from privileged backgrounds. Minority youths, particularly in 1965–1966, served in higher proportion than their percentage of the overall population. Factory neighborhoods, slums, and ghettos, concluded one study, "were the draft boards' happy hunting grounds."

One working-class mother could not understand how "the kids from the fancy suburbs, how they get off when my son has to go over there and maybe get his head shot off." She was right and had only to consider the following random facts:

• a 1965–66 survey revealed that only 2 percent of all draftees were college graduates.[5]

---

[5] This figure increased to about 10 percent by the end of the decade.

- a member of Congress surveyed 100 inductees from his northern Wisconsin district and learned that not one of them came from a family earning more than $5,000 a year.
- of the 1,200 graduates of the Harvard class of 1970, only 56 entered the military and just 2 went to Vietnam.

Once in Vietnam, moreover, draftees were more likely to see combat than those who enlisted voluntarily. A Chicago study, for example, revealed that youths from low-income neighborhoods were three times as likely to die in Vietnam as youths from high-income neighborhoods.

Blacks in and out of the Service Of major concern in the late 1960's was the racial inequity in combat assignments. In 1965, for instance, blacks accounted for 24 percent of all army combat deaths. Although blacks and other minority members continued to do more than their share of the fighting and dying, the Defense Department launched a campaign in 1966 to correct this situation and by the end of the war some progress had been made.

By 1968, however, the nearly 120,000 black Vietnam veterans had become an especially disillusioned group. Black Americans in general were far less likely to support the national effort in Vietnam. In October, 1968, blacks (70 percent) were twice as likely as whites (35 percent) to label themselves doves. Many pointed to the disproportionate numbers of blacks being drafted to fight in Vietnam. Others argued that the huge sums of money being spent in the war effort were being taken from needed domestic programs. Still others, influenced by the black power movement's growing frustration with the slowness of progress in the struggle for equality, did not think their country was worth fighting for. In the late 1960's, riots broke out in the black ghettos of such cities as Detroit, Newark, and Los Angeles, and a shocked nation watched as entire neighborhoods went up in smoke.

Campus Confrontations Meanwhile, as draft calls mounted, so did student protests. On the campuses, "New Left" organizations attracted increased support for their hard-line opposition to the war. During the years 1967–1968, political protests were held in nearly half of all America's 3,000 institutions of higher learning. In some notable cases, such as at Columbia University in New York City, buildings were illegally occupied, property destroyed, and hundreds of students arrested. Overreactions by harrassed police often added to the mounting cycle of disorder and violence.

By the first half of 1969, a study found that about one tenth of all students had taken part in a protest. This number is higher than it might seem when one considers that passive sympathizers usually outnumber the activists.

Impressed with their power, students began making more and more demands on school administrators—who usually gave in to them. They asked for changes in courses of study, insisted on sexual forms of freedom, and demanded that administration policies be eased.

Johnson's Response President Johnson feared that the antiwar movement might turn the public against his policies. As a result, he ordered the CIA to begin spying on antiwar leaders to find out, as he suspected, if they were Communists. Eventually, files on more than 7,000 Americans were drawn up, although no such links with Communists were ever proved. Soon, antiwar leaders were being harrassed. The noted baby doctor, Benjamin Spock, was indicted for having counseled draft resisters. Meanwhile, FBI agents infiltrated peace organizations with the aim of disrupting their work.

The antiwar movement that Johnson so hated started off small, but it was growing rapidly. Although only a small proportion of the population, the doves had among their leaders an unusually articulate number of highly publicized individuals. They included folk singer Joan Baez, boxer Muhammad Ali, actress Jane Fonda, civil rights leader Martin Luther King, Jr., and author Norman Mailer. Increasingly, their movement became connected with a cultural revolution that was sweeping the nation and challenging long-held American values.

The Youth Movement On the campuses and off, the new spirit of opposition and rebellion was creating social divisions. "Don't trust anyone over 30" was a popular slogan of young Americans who were beginning to turn their back on mainstream culture. Some—called hippies—moved to neighborhoods like San Francisco's Haight-Ashbury district or New York City's Greenwich Village where they preached peace and love and stayed stoned.

Indeed, drugs became a symbol of the youth revolt. Marijuana and LSD were the most popular drugs, and their use spread from the more wacked-out rebels into middle-class America. Little about the harmful effects of these drugs was then recognized, with many young people believing that their parents' main drug, alcohol, was far more dangerous. Besides, not everyone claimed to care. A British rock group, The Who, summed up the mood of many young people with their lyrics, "Hope I die before I get old."

THE VIETNAM WAR

The name given to the youthful protests, the drug use, the sit-ins, strikes, marches and other new lifestyles was the **youth movement**. The media was slow to catch on to the impact of this movement. Hollywood, for instance, did not make one anti-Vietnam War film until the fighting was over.[6] Television programming in the 1960's was, to say the least, cautious. Even magazines and newspapers did not know what to think. The *New York Times* called the famous 1969 rock festival at Woodstock a "nightmare of mud and stagnation." "The dreams of marijuana and rock music," the *Times* went on, "had little more sanity than the impulses that drive lemmings to march to the sea."

The music industry, however, was quick to see a profit, and it capitalized on the explosion of music emerging from the youth movement. "Sex, drugs, and rock n' roll," chanted crowds at rock concerts to the shocked disbelief of older Americans. New rock stars burst on to the scene. Jimi Hendrix, Janis Joplin, and Otis Redding all broke through at the first big rock festival, held at Monterey, California in the summer of 1967 (the so-called "summer of love"). Bands playing the new psychedelic rock—such as the Grateful Dead, Jefferson Airplane, and the Doors—also gained amazing popularity.

What all these groups shared with their audiences was a rejection of the goals and values that had led to Vietnam in the first place. Rarely would their songs be political. It was *understood* that they opposed the war; to talk about it would not be cool.

Representatives of mainstream culture decried the youth movement and its hated symbol, rock music. The noted writer William Manchester described rock stars as "short youths, running to fat, who were prepared for public consumption by strenuous dieting, nose surgery, contact lenses, and luxurious hair styles. And they couldn't sing. Most couldn't even have made themselves heard in the back of a theater. Their voices were amplified in echo chambers and then created on tape.... Wiggling their hips and snapping their fingers, their features always fixed in a sullen expression, they would desecrate [destroy] good songs." Such criticism amused young people, reenforcing their belief that they were different, and breaking new ground.

A Look Ahead Student protests, drug use, urban riots—all this represented only a minority of Americans. A majority of Americans continued to support the administration, both in domestic policy and in foreign affairs. But even administration

---

[6.] The only war film of note was *Green Berets,* a John Wayne movie that stridently preached support for the hawk position.

backers were growing wary about Vietnam and were not happy about the turmoil it was causing at home. The national mood by 1967 was best summed up by a homemaker, who told a pollster, "I want to get out, but I don't want to give up."

SECTION 2 REVIEW

1. **Vocabulary to Know** teach-in, Students for a Democratic Society, dove, hawk, draft, exemption, deferment, youth movement

2. What groups constituted the core of the antiwar movement?

3. What effect did the draft have on the antiwar movement?

4. Describe the typical American who was sent to fight in Vietnam.

5. **Critical Thinking** What part did the Vietnam War have in contributing to the growth of the youth movement?

CHAPTER 4 REVIEW

Vocabulary

attrition
battalion days in the field
body count
"Charlie"
Battle of Chu Lai
deferment
defoliant
dove
enclave theory
guns and butter
hearts and minds
morale
pacification
search and destroy
Students for a Democratic
    Society
teach-in
youth movement

Identification

Explain the relationship between the two terms in each of the numbered parts.

1. dove; hawk

2. deferment; exemption

3. attrition; body count

Reviewing the Main Ideas

1. In what ways was the Vietnam War different from other major wars in American history?

2. How did the Communists hope to wear down American morale?

3. Why was the American logistical effort such a major achievement?

4. (a) Why was President Johnson so concerned by the antiwar protests? (b) What actions did he take as a result?

5. What inequities were there in the method of selecting young Americans to fight in Vietnam?

Critical Thinking

Lady Bird Johnson, First Lady during the tumultuous years of the American build-up in Vietnam, was one of her husband's closest advisers and confidants. After her husband died in 1973, she recalled the agony Vietnam caused him. Read the following excerpts from an interview and answer the questions that follow:

> He'd repeat over and over the phrase about the only war this nation wants to wage is the war against poverty, ignorance, and disease, and he took overwhelming pleasure in prosecuting that war.
> But this other quicksand one would not go away ....
> Of course, Lyndon's real fear was not from the left but from the right—people demanding that we get this thing over by dropping—
> *The bomb?*
> —the deadliest of bombs .... He didn't want to be the man ever to have to do it. [H]ow can any President ever, ever give in to that last horrible thing?

1. Which war would Johnson have preferred to fight?

2. What was Johnson's greatest fear?

3. Mrs. Johnson uses the word "quicksand" to describe the war. Why is that word so appropriate?

President Johnson studies a newspaper announcing that
he will not run for re-election.

CHAPTER FIVE

THE TET OFFENSIVE

(1968)

MYRON HARRINGTON, COMMANDER OF A HUNDRED-man marine company, was cautiously leading his troops into Hué. The ancient city was under Communist occupation, and the Americans, having grown accustomed to fighting in rice fields and jungles, had been ordered to clear it. As they came closer, they were reminded of scenes from a World War II movie. Afterwards, Harrington described the city:

> My first impression was of desolation, utter devastation. There were burnt-out tanks and trucks, and upturned automobiles still smoldering. Bodies lay everywhere, most of them civilians. The smoke and stench blended, like in some kind of horror movie.... You felt that something could happen at any minute, that they would jump out and start shooting from every side. Right away I realized that we weren't going to a little picnic.

The battle for Hué was just part of the **Tet offensive** that had engulfed South Vietnam a month before. By the time it was over, about 50,000 Communist troops would be killed, along with 2,000 American and 4,000 South Vietnamese soldiers. But Tet, like the entire Vietnam War, could not be measured in body counts alone.

In this chapter you will read about the Tet offensive and the effect it had on the Vietnam War. As you read, look for answers to the following questions:

1. Why did the Tet offensive stun the United States and South Vietnam?
2. Why were more American troops requested?
3. What led President Johnson to reject a second term?

1 THE TET OFFENSIVE STUNS THE UNITED STATES AND SOUTH VIETNAM

Throughout the later part of 1967, leaders in North Vietnam were preparing for a major offensive in the South. They readied their troops, advising them that the planned "general offensive and uprising" would lead to total victory.

Communist Strategy General Giap, in charge of the operation, had complicated reasons for planning the offensive. Like his American counterparts, Giap recognized that the war was deadlocked. Although he was fully prepared to fight for as many years as necessary to unify Vietnam, he thought the time was ripe to put immediate pressure on the United States. He suspected, and rightly, that American resources were being stretched thin. He hoped, first of all, that he could force the United States to the bargaining table—on his terms—and get the Americans to stop bombing North Vietnam.

Giap had a second reason for organizing the Tet offensive: he wanted to break down the alliance between the Americans and the South Vietnamese. Giap believed that there was widespread resentment against the Americans in South Vietnam, and that the population, ripe for revolution, was ready to rise up against the foreigners on their soil. Many of the attacks during Tet would be aimed at American targets, including the United States embassy in Saigon, as if to demonstrate to the South Vietnamese people that the Americans were not all-powerful. Giap planned, then, to try to influence South Vietnamese opinion, not American opinion. As it turned out, just the opposite would take place.

Attacks in the Central Highlands Before Tet started, a series of Communist attacks on isolated American outposts in the central highlands occupied center stage. The Vietcong and North Vietnamese losses were staggering, for in these conventional

THE TET OFFENSIVE (1968)

attacks the Americans could call in enormous firepower. In the battle at Con Thien, a small marine fire base located just south of the North Vietnamese border, almost 800 B-52 flights dropped 22,000 tons of bombs on the attackers.

Soon an even larger battle was raging around nearby **Khe Sanh.** At first the site of a small Special Forces camp, Khe Sanh was later planned as a forward base for attacks against Communist sanctuaries in Laos and had been strengthened by a marine battalion. Later in 1967, as intelligence reports indicated that as many as 40,000 North Vietnamese troops were preparing to assault Khe Sanh, Westmoreland ordered 6,000 marines into place. He also directed that the use of tactical nuclear weapons be studied, a proposal Washington banned out of concern about protests at home.

Fears of Another Dienbienphu Was another Dienbienphu in the making? The comparison with the French disaster at first seemed logical, for both sites were isolated outposts under heavy siege. Johnson, for one, was determined that there be no repeat of Dienbienphu and that the American positions be held at all costs. He even went so far as to insist that the Joint Chiefs sign a formal document declaring their faith in Westmoreland's ability to defend Khe Sanh.

Actually, there were important differences between Khe Sanh and Dienbienphu. The American position at Khe Sanh was a stronger one than that at Dienbienphu, and more easily defended. The marines commanded most of the hills surrounding their base, while the French had held no high ground. In addition, the American airstrip remained open throughout the battle, while the French runway had been closed on the first day of the siege. Finally, the Americans had far more aircraft at their disposal than the French, particularly the mighty B-52's.[1] This firepower would prove to be decisive.

Meanwhile, the marines waited for the expected attack. They talked and sang, played cards and listened to music, and shot rats for target practice. The Communists inched nearer, digging trenches as close as 300 yards of the base perimeter. Tanks were even brought down from the North. A marine described the mood of the camp. "Being in Khe Sanh," he said, "is like sitting in an electric chair and waiting for someone to pull the switch."

[1.] Over the nine-week siege of Khe Sanh, B-52's would drop more than 75,000 tons of explosives—the most firepower ever dropped on a single target in the history of warfare.

The Siege of Khe Sanh On January 2, 1968, six North Vietnamese officers dressed in marine uniforms were shot as they tried to penetrate Khe Sanh's barbed wire fence. The attack had begun. In the days and weeks that followed, the Communists made repeated suicide charges against Khe Sanh, with some units suffering casualties at the rate of 90 percent.

By early March the North Vietnamese decided to withdraw. During the two-month siege, they had lost as many as 10,000 soldiers, with fewer than 500 marines killed. But why had they been willing to stage the doomed attack in the first place? Many observers believe that the Communists wanted to draw American attention away from the towns and cities of South Vietnam, where deadly surprise attacks were about to take place. If so, their strategy worked. Westmoreland put all his energy into the defense of Khe Sanh, believing that reports about attacks on population centers were mere **diversions** (maneuvers to draw the attention of an enemy away from the planned point of attack).

Anticipating Trouble Actually, American experts suspected that something was about to happen. Information gained from captured documents, prisoners, and secret agents suggested that, as Westmoreland alerted Washington on December 20, 1967, a "maximum effort" by Communist forces could be expected. General **Earle Wheeler,** chairman of the Joint Chiefs, agreed, warning that "it is entirely possible there may be a Communist thrust similar to the desperate effort of the Germans in the Battle of the Bulge in World War II."

But knowing what exactly was going to happen—and where—was hard to determine. Westmoreland expected the main enemy effort to be in the northern provinces, and he rushed extra troops to the region. He also thought the main action would come before Tet.

The Tet Surprise The Vietnamese New Year holiday, Tet was traditionally a time of celebration, a time when warring parties would respect a cease-fire truce. Now, on the eve of Tet, came a secret order to attack. The following poem, written by Ho Chi Minh to mark the start of the Year of the Monkey, signalled the beginning of the Communist offensive:

> This Spring far outshines the previous Springs,
> Of Victories throughout the land come happy tidings.
> Let North and South emulate each other in fighting
>   the U.S. aggressors!
> Forward!
> Total Victory will be ours.

THE TET OFFENSIVE (1968)

In the days leading up to Tet, the Communists had prepared themselves for the surprise attack. Vietcong guerrillas, often disguised as ARVN soldiers, moved into the cities and towns. Weapons were smuggled in on wagons and carts and even in fake funeral processions.

Some 80,000 Communist soldiers went into action on the evening of January 30, 1968. A number of North Vietnamese regulars, expecting to lose their lives, put on armbands, with the words "Born in the North, Died in the South."

The attackers struck at more than 100 towns and cities, including Saigon. No fewer than 36 of 44 provincial capitals were hit, as were 64 district towns, countless villages, and 12 United States bases (including Danang, Camranh Bay, and other coastal locations until then thought safe from attack).

The Americans and South Vietnamese had been caught off guard. For the first time, the Communists had dared to enter the cities in force. For the first time, they had coordinated their military planning on a countrywide scale. For the first time, they had committed large numbers of troops to a single campaign.

In their boldest move, over 4,000 Communist troops struck at carefully selected sites in the South Vietnamese capital. During more than twenty years of fighting, Saigon had been relatively secure. Now, General Westmoreland's headquarters were bombarded, as were those of the South Vietnamese general staff offices. The main radio station was occupied too.

A key objective in Saigon was the United States embassy, symbol of the American presence. Nineteen commandos, on a suicide mission, blasted a hole in the wall surrounding the heavily fortified but lightly defended embassy compound. Unable to get into the embassy itself, the attackers took cover behind large concrete flower pots and fired at the building. That evening, shocked Americans watched television coverage of the battle to clear the embassy grounds. Only after six hours of action were the commandos overpowered and the embassy secured.

Atrocities During the attacks, the Communists were uncommonly brutal, slaughtering anyone they labeled an enemy—including harmless minor officials, teachers, and doctors. The worst atrocities took place in Hué. While the Communists had control of the city, they ordered all civil servants, military personnel, and those who had worked for the Americans to report to specially designated locations (including the city's Catholic cathedral). From 3,000 to 5,000 of those who dutifully obeyed the order were killed, their bodies found in mass graves after American and South Vietnamese forces retook the city.

The South Vietnamese often responded in kind. In one

unforgettable scene the chief of the national police, Colonel Nguyen Ngoc Loan, was filmed on a Saigon street as he held a gun to the head of a Vietcong suspect and then pulled the trigger. NBC television broadcast the shocking execution, only slightly edited, to millions of American homes.

VIETNAM FACT

Tet came as such a surprise to the American people because by late 1967 military and political leaders were sounding more hopeful than ever about the war. Army chief of Staff Harold Johnson perceived a "smell of success," Secretary of State Rusk described the enemy as "hurting very badly," and General Westmoreland said, "We have reached an important point when the end begins to come into view." Perhaps the most optimistic of all the administration figures was Vice President Humphrey. Casting caution aside, he asserted, "We are beginning to win this struggle. We are on the offensive. Territory is being gained. We are making steady progress."

The Impact of Tet By February 1, General Westmoreland had concluded that the enemy offensive "is about to run out of steam." The next day, President Johnson announced in a press conference that the Tet offensive was a "complete failure." He went on to make a number of statement so clearly false that his most loyal friends and supporters were said to be worried.

In a military sense, however, Westmoreland and Johnson were probably right. In most instances, the Communists were swiftly crushed, and by the end of the first week of fighting, the great majority of cities and towns were back in government hands. (Communist forces did hold out longer in a least a dozen places, however, including Hué[2] and parts of Saigon.) Stretched thin by the country-wide effort, the attackers were not able to stand up to the superior American and South Vietnamese firepower. They had

---

[2.] With more than 50 percent of the city destroyed or damaged, leaving the great majority of its residents homeless, Hué would never be the same. Its very name would evoke memories of death and destruction. An observer described the once-beautiful city as "a shattered, stinking hulk, its streets choked with rubble and rotting bodies."

THE TET OFFENSIVE (1968)

failed to touch off, furthermore, the expected popular uprising against the Americans. Among those most disappointed by Tet were the Vietcong. In the forefront of the fighting, the Vietcong suffered devastating losses and would be replaced and dominated in the years to come by Communists from the North.

And yet South Vietnam had been greatly battered too. As a result of Tet, more than a half million additional people had been forced from their homes, and now one of every twelve South Vietnamese was a **refugee**, living in overcrowded camps and adding to the strain on an economy that could ill afford it. There were as many as 38,000 civilian casualties, many of them killed by American bombs, particularly in Saigon where planes pounded Vietcong positions for two weeks in some of the most heavily populated sections of the city. Many people angrily blamed the Communists, but others criticized the United States and the Saigon government for destroying their homes. Looting by South Vietnamese soldiers during the fighting added to the bitter feelings.

Perhaps the greatest impact of Tet, however, would be felt in the United States. Television coverage had brought the Tet offensive into the homes of the American people, and the American people were about to render their own verdict about the Vietnam War.

SECTION 1 REVIEW

1. **Vocabulary to Know** Tet offensive, Khe Sanh, diversion, refugee

2. **People to Identify** Earle Wheeler

3. Why did General Giap decide to launch the Tet offensive?

4. (a) For what reason did the Communists attack Khe Sanh? (b) What were the results?

5. Why did the Tet attacks come as a surprise?

6. What were the main Communist targets during Tet?

7. **Critical Thinking** Why was Johnson so determined not to allow Khe Sanh to turn into another Dienbienphu?

2 MORE AMERICAN TROOPS ARE REQUESTED

For months and then years, the public had been told that the war in Vietnam was going well and that victory was fast approaching. Yet, well before the Tet offensive, doubts about America's role in Southeast Asia had been growing. More and more people had concluded that it had been a mistake to send troops to Vietnam in the first place. Many were discouraged, furthermore, believing that once there, the troops had not been allowed to win the war. In spite of the vocal "pro-peace" protesters, a majority of Americans supported a policy tougher than the one pursued by the administration. But now, after Tet, the public had lost all confidence in President Johnson's ability to provide the leadership to get the job done.

Johnson's Reaction to Tet Like most Americans, Johnson had never imagined that the Communists in South Vietnam would be strong or daring enough to attack the cities or assault the United States embassy in Saigon. He had come to believe the rosy reports he had demanded, and now he was stunned. He quickly recognized Tet's impact, however, particularly when such trustworthy figures as Walter Cronkite—America's favorite newsman—predicted on his nationally televised broadcast that it seemed "more certain than ever that the bloody experience in Vietnam is to end in a stalemate." Soon, Johnson would have new worries. The military was calling for more troops.

Troop Requests On February 8, while fighting was still raging in Hué, Earle Wheeler had cabled General Westmoreland, stating "If you need more troops, ask for them." In urging Westmoreland to make the request, the chairman of the Joint Chiefs was using the Tet emergency to force the President to make a difficult decision. He wanted Johnson to call up the **reserves**. (The reserves are that part of a country's armed forces not on active duty but subject to call in an emergency.)

Throughout the Vietnam War, Johnson had resisted mobilizing the reserves. As a result, the troop build-up in Vietnam had been accompanied by a weakening of American military strength in the rest of the world. Bases in Europe were severely understaffed. The United States itself was defended by units only one third their normal size. The draft could only go so far in meeting the military's needs. Draftees lacked necessary skills, and already demonstrations against compulsory service were mounting.

Westmoreland, in agreeing to Wheeler's suggestion, sounded

THE TET OFFENSIVE (1968)

a note of alarm. "I desperately need reinforcements," he wrote the President. "Time is of the essence."

Johnson recognized immediately that sending more troops to Vietnam would require him to call 100,000 army and marine reservists to service. But now Westmoreland, at Wheeler's suggestion, drew up a more specific request to cover the responsibilities of the United States not only in Vietnam but in the rest of the world as well. The plan called for 206,000 men, roughly half of whom would be sent to Vietnam by May 1. The remainder would be sent later in the year, if needed, or they would be assigned to other locations.

To back up Westmoreland's request, Wheeler reported to Johnson that Tet had been a "very near thing" and that similar disasters were a possibility. More troops must be sent to Vietnam, he insisted—which, again, meant calling up the reserves.

Clark Clifford's Advice The choices facing the President were agonizing. To meet the new request for troops, he would have to place the nation on a war footing. Presidential elections were fast approaching, and Johnson did not want to have to run as a "war" candidate. To turn down the request, however, would be to risk defeat on the battlefield.

To help him decide what to do, Johnson turned to his new Secretary of Defense, **Clark Clifford**. A backer of the administration's policy in Vietnam from the beginning, Clifford had been named to the Cabinet because Johnson felt he would provide him with more steadfast support than Robert McNamara. Johnson would soon learn, however, that Clifford had gradually—and quietly—turned against the war. After a series of meetings with top military officials, he had become convinced that the nation was following a dangerous policy. No one could tell him how many more troops might be needed after the 206,000 then being requested. No one could see an alternative to the long, grinding war that was intended, at some unknown point, to wear down the North Vietnamese.

In a report he prepared for the President, Clifford bluntly stated that there was no proof that "an additional 200,000 American troops, or double or triple that quantity" could defeat the Communists. Instead, he hinted that American forces should cease their "search and destroy" missions and withdraw to well-protected positions—including the major cities—along the coast.

A Decision Postponed Johnson, who had been on the verge of granting the troop request, received Clifford's report without enthusiasm. He decided, however, to put off making a decision and instructed his press secretary to say, less than honestly, that "no specific requests" for troops had reached him. At the same time, news of the request had begun to spread on Capitol Hill, and antiwar leaders, such as Robert Kennedy, denounced the proposal on the Senate floor. Senators Henry Jackson and John Stennis, who had once fully backed all requests from the military, were also disturbed. They sensed that the war could not be won so long as the present strategy was being followed. They too would oppose further troops deployments.

SECTION 2 REVIEW

1. **Vocabulary to Know** reserves

2. **People to Identify** Clark Clifford

3. (a) Why did military leaders want to call up the reserves? (b) Why was Johnson reluctant to do so?

4. What advice did Clark Clifford give the President regarding Vietnam?

5. **Critical Thinking** What was the chief impact of Tet?

3 JOHNSON REJECTS A SECOND TERM

Soon the media was breaking news of the troop requests too, and the stories could not have come at a worse time for the President. The first presidential primary would be held in New Hampshire in mid-March, and although Johnson hadn't formally announced his decision to seek re-election, observers assumed that he would run again in November. His name was not on the New Hampshire ballot, but a write-in campaign was being carried on for him, with advertisements warning voters that "The Communists in Vietnam are watching the New Hampshire primary."

A Surprise in New Hampshire Opposing the President was **Eugene McCarthy,** a senator from Minnesota who was virtually unknown nationally. A strong opponent of the war, McCarthy had entered the race only to mount a symbolic challenge to the incumbent President. In other words, he had no thought of actually winning the nomination.

Polls taken just two weeks before Election Day had shown

THE TET OFFENSIVE (1968)

McCarthy capturing less than 20 percent of the vote. But when the ballots were counted in New Hampshire, a major shift in voter opinion was revealed. McCarthy had come close to defeating the President, finishing second by only 300 votes out of the 50,000 votes cast. The uproar that followed was so great that most Americans assumed that McCarthy *had* won. Just to come so near was a breakthrough in American politics, for opposing the nomination of a President from one's own party, as McCarthy was doing, was virtually unprecedented.

Another Candidate for President Four days later, Johnson received more bad news. Another candidate had entered the race, and this time it was someone who presented an even more serious challenge. The candidate was **Robert Kennedy.** As brother of the slain President, Kennedy evoked warm public memories of the glamour and confidence of the early 1960's, when Vietnam was still a far-off problem and American optimism was at its height. Along with McCarthy, Kennedy was a passionate "peace" candidate, forcing Johnson into a position he disliked—that of being the "war" candidate.

Advice from the "Wise Men" Johnson's first reaction to these political setbacks was to stand tough. "The time has come," he told a Minneapolis audience, "when we ought to ... support our leaders, our government, our men, and our allies until aggression is stopped, wherever it has occurred." But another primary would soon be held—this time in Wisconsin, on April 2—and the beleaguered President recognized the need to do something dramatic.

As a first step, he told Westmoreland that he would send him just 13,500 troops, and no more. In addition, the Saigon regime would have to make a greater effort.[3] Then, as he had done so often in the past, he called in a group of respected American statesmen, many of whom had participated in making Vietnam policy.

Almost all the "wise men" who Johnson called together in late March had endorsed his policies just five months before. But that was before Tet, and no fewer than nine of the fourteen participants had now turned against the war.

The most respected of them was Dean Acheson, who had talked Truman into financing the French effort in Vietnam twenty years earlier (page 17). Acheson now argued that the Saigon government would never gain popular support and that, as a

---

[3.] Only after Tet did South Vietnam begin to draft eighteen-year-olds, something the United States had been doing for three years.

result, the war could never be won. The United States, in short, had to find a way out of Vietnam.

The advice of the "wise men" dismayed the President but moved him to action too. In his memoirs he wrote, "If they had been so deeply influenced by the reports of the Tet offensive, what must the average person in the country be thinking?"

Johnson's Withdrawal What, though, would the President do? Earlier, plans had been made for Johnson to speak to the nation about Vietnam on March 31. The televised speech would clearly be an important one, and several of his advisers submitted drafts for his approval. As the date approached, and as more and more drafts littered the speechwriters' desks, no one was sure what move the President would make. A partial halt to the bombing of North Vietnam would be announced, but Johnson made it clear that he was unhappy with the end of the speech. He would write his own ending, he told his staff. And then he went to rehearse his speech thoroughly on videotape. He wanted it to be perfect, for he knew it would be remembered as the most famous speech he ever gave.

On the night of March 31, 1968, the nation watched as Johnson began with the words "I want to talk to you about peace in Vietnam." He announced the bombing halt (except in areas where the North Vietnamese were continuing to build up troops and supplies) and he offered to open negotiations with the Communists. But it was the close of his address that startled the viewing audience. The man who just four years earlier had won one of the greatest electoral victories in American political history now told the nation of his decision to withdraw from the presidential race. In grim tones, he read:

> I have concluded that I should not permit the presidency to become involved in the partisan divisions that are developing in this political year .... Accordingly, I shall not seek, and I will not accept, the nomination of my party for another term as your President.

Much was made of Johnson's surprise decision, though many factors surely contributed to it. In the speech, Johnson spoke of the good of the country, suggesting that he had stepped out of the race to emphasize his sincerity about wanting to end the war. Predictions that he might not win renomination no doubt influenced him too. So did his private fears about the state of his health. He had suffered a serious heart attack in 1955 and was aware of the strain that he was under. He would, in fact, die of a heart attack a little more than five years later.

THE TET OFFENSIVE (1968)

Peace Talks Begin Many people assumed that peace would soon be reached, and three days after Johnson's speech the North Vietnamese agreed to begin talks to end the war. The conference opened in Paris on May 10, 1968, amid high hopes. But then, as the weeks dragged on, it became apparent that a settlement lay far in the future. The North refused to withdraw its troops from South Vietnam, while the United States objected to including Vietcong representatives in the Saigon government. (One American declared that such a move would be like "putting the fox in a chicken coop.")

The talks would continue for five long years—and with them, so would the fighting. The spring of 1968, in fact, saw the United States step up its military operations in Vietnam. The number of B-52 missions tripled in 1968, and the largest search-and-destroy missions of the war were conducted. "Charlie is being relentlessly pursued night and day and pounded to shreds whenever and wherever we catch him," reported one American officer. The war went on.

VIETNAM FACT

On June 13, 1968, Vietnam became this country's longest war—longer than the Revolutionary War, the Civil War, World Wars I and II, or Korea. Americans had been fighting and dying in Vietnam for six-and-a-half years, ever since December 22, 1961, when an army private was killed by Vietcong bullets in a Mekong Delta ambush. And the fighting was by no means over.

SECTION 3 REVIEW

1. **People to Identify** Eugene McCarthy, Robert Kennedy

2. (a) What was the outcome of the New Hampshire primary? (b) Why was the result a surprise? (c) What other candidate then entered the race?

3. What advice did the "wise men" give Johnson?

4. **Critical Thinking** Why was Johnson's decision not to seek another term such a shock?

CHAPTER 5 REVIEW

Vocabulary and People

Clark Clifford
diversion
Robert Kennedy
Eugene McCarthy
Khe Sanh

refugee
reserves
Tet offensive
Earle Wheeler

Identification

Write the numbered sentences on a separate sheet of paper. In each sentence fill in the blank, using one of the words from the list above.

1. Following the _____, the military asked for 206,000 more troops to be sent to Vietnam.

2. Throughout the war, President Johnson resisted calling up the _____ to meet American manpower needs.

3. The large number of people forced by the fighting to seek safety moved to _____ camps, putting a strain on the South Vietnamese economy.

4. The surprise showing of _____ in the New Hampshire primary stunned President Johnson.

5. _____, a close adviser to Johnson, urged that the administration find a way out of the Vietnam War.

Reviewing the Main Ideas

1. What part did Khe Sanh play in the Communists' Tet strategy?

2. What was unusual about the Communists' targets during the Tet offensive?

3. What impact did Tet have on each of the following? (a) The Vietcong (b) South Vietnam (c) The American public

THE TET OFFENSIVE (1968)

4. (a) What was Walter Cronkite's analysis of Tet? (b) Why did that view concern Johnson?

5. What effect did the Vietnam War have on America's worldwide military strength?

Critical Thinking

In his memoirs, General Westmoreland recalled the impact of Tet. Read the following passage and then answer the questions that follow:

> Nobody in Saigon to my knowledge anticipated remotely the psychological impact the offensive would have in the United States. Militarily, the offensive was foredoomed to failure, destined to be over everywhere, except in Saigon and Hué and at Khe Sanh, in a day or so, certainly nothing to compare with the six weeks required to defeat and eliminate the gains of the Battle of the Bulge or with the violence and extensive gains of the Chinese Communists' onslaught in Korea. The American people absorbed those psychological blows with little [difficulty]. No one to my knowledge foresaw that, in terms of public opinion, press and television would transform what was undeniably a catastrophic military defeat for the enemy into a presumed debacle [disaster] for Americans and South Vietnamese, an attitude that still lingers in the minds of many.

1. (a) What, according to Westmoreland, was the military impact of Tet? (b) What did he believe was the impact of Tet on the American public? (c) Who does he blame for the public's opinion of Tet?

2. (a) With what previous military campaigns does Westmoreland compare Tet? (b) When did those campaigns take place? (c) How did media coverage differ in those years from the coverage of Tet?

3. How do Westmoreland's words underscore the close relation between the military effort and public opinion?

U.S. planes bomb fuel storage area near Hanoi.

CHAPTER SIX

NIXON AND THE WAR

(1969–1973)

AS AMERICANS LOOK BACK, THEY USUALLY associate the Vietnam War with Lyndon Johnson. Indeed, the commitment to fight in Vietnam, along with the massive troop build-up, was mainly Johnson's responsibility. Johnson's departure from the White House, however, did not bring peace to Southeast Asia. In fact, the war dragged on for five long years, and more Americans lost their lives in Vietnam during those years than had been killed during the Johnson era. In addition, opposition to the war at home grew to a point where it threatened to tear the nation apart.

In this chapter you will read about Richard Nixon's long and painful search for an American withdrawal from Vietnam. You will read too about the wrenching effect the continuing war had on American society and on the American military. As you read, look for answers to the following questions:

1. **What changes did the new administration bring to Vietnam policies?**
2. **Why did the United States invade Cambodia?**
3. **What progress was made in ending the war?**

1 A NEW ADMINISTRATION TAKES OFFICE AND SEARCHES FOR A SOLUTION TO THE VIETNAM WAR

The man who led the nation during these tumultuous years was **Richard Nixon**. Having fallen into obscurity after his unsuccessful presidential race against John Kennedy in 1960 and his defeat in a California gubernatorial contest two years later, Nixon made a dramatic political comeback in 1968. He handily captured the Republican nomination for President,[1] and then faced the appealing prospect of running against the badly divided Democrats.

A longtime supporter of American involvement in Vietnam, Nixon nevertheless pledged, during the 1968 presidential campaign, to "end the war and win the peace." He even talked of having a "secret plan" to halt the bloodshed, and this won him valuable attention. He said he did not want to reveal his plan, however, so as not to upset the peace talks then going on in Paris.[2]

The Democratic Convention of 1968 The Democrats, meanwhile, were set to choose a candidate for President at their convention in Chicago. Before the delegates arrived, the city was transformed into an armed camp. Fearing huge antiwar demonstrations, Chicago's powerful major, **Richard Daley,** had ringed the convention hall with thousands of police and fire fighters, while thousands more national guardsmen and regular army troops waited nervously for the word to go into action.

The masses of violent protesters never appeared, but there was a youthful crowd that numbered more than 10,000. Ignoring the mayor's ban against large gatherings, the demonstrators assembled at a downtown location, Grant Park, in front of a hotel where many convention delegates were staying.

As the crisis was brewing in the streets, tempers inside the convention hall were running almost as high. Robert Kennedy had been assassinated in June, leaving the antiwar forces without a strong contender. It was clear that Vice President **Hubert Humphrey,** a loyal administration member since 1964, would win the nomination. As a result, antiwar delegates focused their energy on the Vietnam plank in the party's platform. They submitted a document calling for the withdrawal of American troops from Vietnam and the establishment of a coalition government in

---

[1] Governor George Romney of Michigan, the leading Republican contender at the start of the campaign, had destroyed his chances when he charged that he had been "brainwashed" by administration officials during a 1965 visit to Vietnam.

[2] Nixon's "secret plan" turned out mainly to be campaign rhetoric.

NIXON AND THE WAR (1969–1973)

Saigon. After impassioned debate, the plank was rejected by a vote of 1,567 to 1,041. Still, fully 40 percent of the delegates had refused to endorse the policies of their own President.

Meanwhile, the mood at Grant Park was ugly. After being pelted with bricks and bottles, the police struck back at the demonstrators. Television cameras recorded the bloody riot that followed, sending images of violence into the homes of an incredulous nation. "The whole world is watching!" chanted the protesters as the police, their pent-up anger spilling over, attacked anyone who crossed their path—demonstrators, reporters, and innocent bystanders alike.

Two months later the Johnson-appointed **Walker Commission** would criticize the Daley administration, calling the Chicago events a "police riot." Humphrey, for his part, won his party's nomination but now faced an uphill battle. "I felt when we left that convention we were in an impossible situation," he later said. "Chicago was a catastrophe.... I told [my wife] I felt just like we had been in a shipwreck."

The Election of 1968 The Democrats never fully recovered from Chicago. Even though President Johnson helped Humphrey's chances by announcing a halt to all air, naval, and artillery bombardment of North Vietnam just a week before the election, many doves refused to support the Democrats. The party was further hurt by the candidacy of **George Wallace.** The Alabama governor proved successful in attracting the support of many working-class Americans, once Democrats, who believed that no one was standing up for "little guy." Wallace would rouse audiences with his attacks on "briefcase-totin' bureaucrats, ivory-tower guideline writers, bearded anarchists, smart-aleck editorial writers, and pointy-headed professors."

In November, Nixon scored a narrow victory. Out of nearly 73 million ballots cast, his winning margin was fewer than 500,000 votes. In the electoral college, Nixon's margin was wider: 301 votes to Humphrey's 191 and Wallace's 46.

Nixon and Foreign Affairs Nixon came to office determined to break new ground in foreign policy. Once passionately opposed to any contact with the Chinese Communists, for example, he had come to the conclusion, in 1967, that China could no longer be left "outside the family of nations, to live in angry isolation." With China and the Soviet Union now bitter rivals, Nixon saw an opportunity for the United States to win concessions from the Communist giants. He looked forward to opening talks with both countries. But how would he go about it? And how, more to the immediate point, would he deal with Vietnam?

To assist him, Nixon named **Henry Kissinger** as his national security adviser. Kissinger was a Harvard professor who, only months before, had called Nixon "the most dangerous, of all the men running, to have as President." But Kissinger was motivated by an all-consuming ambition, and he quickly accepted Nixon's surprising offer of a White House position, understanding its potential for power. It was soon clear that Nixon, distrustful of the State Department, wanted the White House to be the center of authority in the making of foreign policy. Symbolic of the new approach was the fact that Nixon named Kissinger to his post before choosing either a Secretary of Defense or Secretary of State.

Vietnam Strategy Both Nixon and Kissinger shared certain assumptions about Vietnam. Acknowledging the impact of Tet on the American public, they agreed that the administration was limited in what it could do. In short, a negotiated settlement was needed to bring an "honorable" end to the war.

How, though, could such a settlement be reached? Both believed that more force could pressure the North Vietnamese into agreeing to a settlement. For Nixon, North Vietnamese concessions were essential, for he did not want to abandon South Vietnam completely. Kissinger, on the other hand, supported a settlement that would simply "buy time" for the Saigon government, giving it a "reasonable" chance to survive.

Tet '69 As much as Nixon and Kissinger would have liked to debate strategy, the realities of the battlefield soon made themselves apparent. On February 22, 1969, the day after the end of the Tet cease-fire, the Communists launched attacks thoughout the length of Vietnam. The attacks of **Tet '69** were different, however, from the Tet offensive of the year before. Because American forces were better able to screen the countryside for the large-scale movement of Communist forces, the enemy avoided major attacks. In another difference, the Communists also avoided attacking civilian populations. Instead, their goal was to hit American military installations and inflict as many casualties on United States troops as possible. By the time the offensive had run its course, well over 1,000 Americans had lost their lives.

Communist Bases in Cambodia Nixon was determined to repay the Communists for Tet '69. He also wanted to get his presidency off to a vigorous start. The only way to force the North

NIXON AND THE WAR (1969-1973)

Vietnamese to negotiate seriously, he told his top aides on March 16, 1969, was "to do something on the military front, something they will understand." However, he did not want to sabotage the Paris peace talks by resuming the bombing of North Vietnam. He decided instead that Cambodia should be struck.

The ruler of Cambodia, **Prince Norodom Sihanouk,** had tried to keep his nation neutral since it won independence from France in 1954. Playing up to whomever he felt could offer him the most protection—first the United States, then China—he had ended by allowing the Vietnamese Communists to operate in the parts of Cambodia closest to South Vietnam. Throughout the Vietnam War, then, Communist forces would routinely attack South Vietnamese targets and then retreat across the border to safety in Cambodia.

Sihanouk was never happy with the Communist bases on his soil, however, because over the centuries the Vietnamese had frequently invaded Cambodia and were that land's traditional enemy. Late in 1967, the prince shifted his policy and granted American forces in South Vietnam the right of "hot pursuit" against Communists retreating to Cambodia, as long as no Cambodians were injured.

Nothing came of Sihanouk's "hot pursuit" offer while Johnson was in office. Within a week of Nixon's inauguration, however, General **Creighton Abrams,** named as Westmoreland's successor in the spring of 1968, learned that as many as 40,000 Communist troops had recently moved into the Cambodian bases. Abrams recommended that B-52's be sent in to raid the Communist sanctuaries. Since he claimed—falsely—that no civilians were in the area, the raids could be considered as falling under Sihanouk's "hot pursuit" restriction.

The Bombing of Cambodia Late in March, 1969, Nixon agreed to the bombing of Cambodia. The raids would continue for fourteen months, and they were carried out in total secrecy. Nixon and Kissinger feared that if news of the bombing were made public, violent antiwar demonstrations would break out at home and there would be an international outcry as well. By keeping silent they were also able to make things easier for Sihanouk. The prince could still publicly claim that he was neutral, while privately he could use the Americans to strike at the Vietnamese on his soil. (Indeed, Cambodia's army provided the United States with information about the Communist bases.) The North Vietnamese, for their part, remained silent too, not wanting to admit that their troops were in Cambodia in the first place.

As part of the secret campaign, Congress was not told of the bombing—and not even the Secretary of the Air Force or the Air Force Chief of Staff were fully informed. A news story did break in May, however, leading Nixon to have wiretaps placed on the telephones of certain officials, including members of Kissinger's staff. This use of dubious methods to find out what Nixon's "enemies" were doing would later end in the Watergate scandal. The secret bombing, officially revealed in 1973, would also be one of the impeachment charges leveled against Nixon in the events leading up to his resignation from office.

Vietnamization The Cambodian bombing made no difference to the talks going on in Paris. Knowing that time was on their side, the Communists' only goal was to wait until the Americans left South Vietnam.

Soon, there were indications that the Americans would be leaving. Nixon, under intense domestic pressure, was advancing a plan that came to be called **Vietnamization.** Under the plan, the size of the South Vietnamese armed forces, about 850,000 when Nixon took office, was enlarged to more than 1 million. In addition, the United States turned over to South Vietnam huge quantities of weapons, ships, planes, helicopters—and enough vehicles to make one observer ask if the purpose was to "put every South Vietnamese soldier behind the wheel." In addition, a shield of American B-52's and other planes could be called in at any time in case of Communist attack. The United States, meanwhile, planned to pull out its combat forces while the South Vietnamese army, strengthened by advisers and equipment, would be trained to replace them.[3]

Another part of Vietnamization was an effort to bring new life into rural development programs. Village elections were held, restoring self-government for the first time since before the days of Diem. An ambitious land reform program distributed nearly a million hectares to peasants, and efforts were made to build schools, repair bridges, and clear roads.

Vietnamization would enable Nixon to remove American forces from Vietnam while allowing him to claim that he had not "lost" the nation's first war. The success of the plan, however, was far from assured. For all the activity in the countryside, there was no great evidence of grass-roots support for the Saigon government. The withdrawal of American troops, meanwhile, went slowly at first. Following a meeting in June, 1969, between

---

[3.] New equipment to help spot troop movements—including portable radar units, various devices that could detect body heat, and even "people sniffers," which picked up the scent of human urine—eased the burden of having to send out large numbers of troops on patrol.

Presidents Nixon and Thieu on the Pacific island of Midway, the withdrawal of a token 25,000 Americans was announced. Following this first step, however, Secretary of Defense **Melvin Laird** eagerly drew up a plan that would reduce United States troop strength in Vietnam to 206,000 by the end of 1971.

Kissinger, for one, had doubts about a speedy withdrawal from Vietnam. He argued that the American troops served as a useful bargaining chip at the Paris peace talks. He believed too that the South Vietnamese would be hard-pressed to replace the departing Americans. Kissinger now called for "savage punishment" against the North. "I can't believe," he told his staff, "that a fourth-rate power like North Vietnam doesn't have a breaking point."

Deadlocked Peace Talks Part of the administration's frustration came from the fact that the Paris peace talks were going nowhere. After their opening in 1968, in fact, the talks had quickly turned into a tragic farce, with the main debate having to do with the shape of the conference table. In August, Kissinger met secretly in Paris with the chief North Vietnamese delegate, Xuan Thuy. Nothing was resolved. The North Vietnamese refused to withdraw their troops from South Vietnam, while the United States refused to allow Communist participation in the South Vietnamese government. In a secret message to Ho Chi Minh, Nixon turned to threats. He would order new bombing raids on North Vietnam, he said, unless a diplomatic breakthrough were achieved by November 1, 1969.

The Death of Ho Chi Minh Ho's response reached Washington on August 30, 1969, and in it he promised nothing new. Three days later, he died at the age of 79. His death had the effect of toughening the resolve of the North Vietnamese. His successors had been fighting against Westerners for most of their lives, and more than ever they now regarded the defeat of the United States as their sacred duty. There seemed little chance that they would agree to a compromise.

Antiwar Momentum The confidence of American hawks, on the other hand, was weakening. In September, Charles Goodell, a Republican senator from New York, proposed legislation in Congress to bring home all the GI's by the end of 1970. Ten similar resolutions were introduced in the next three weeks, and though none passed, the pressure on Nixon to end the war was becoming intense.

Across the country, meanwhile, antiwar activists were

planning a series of peaceful demonstrations called **moritoriums.** Organized mainly by moderate political veterans of the McCarthy and Kennedy campaigns, the demonstrations were intended to call for a moritorium (that is, a halt) on "business as usual" until the war was ended. Protest rallies were scheduled in communities across the United States, rather than just on college campuses.

On the first moritorium, held on October 15, 1969, huge crowds gathered in Washington, New York, Boston, Miami, and other cities to listen to antiwar speakers. The peaceful demonstrations, in contrast to the violence of Chicago, had religious overtones. Nationwide, church bells tolled, while the names of American dead were read at candlelight services. An estimated 1 million people took part, and for the first time the demonstrators were as likely to wear business suits as jeans. In Vietnam, small numbers of American servicemen wore black armbands in sympathy, an indication that antiwar sentiment had started to spread into the armed forces.

Vice President **Spiro Agnew** blasted the demonstrators as "an effete corps of impudent snobs." He called them "malcontents, radicals, incendiaries, and civil and uncivil disobedients," and said, "I would swap the whole damn zoo for a single platoon of the kind of Americans I saw in Vietnam." Nixon, while avoiding such heated phrases, let it be known that he would never be influenced by public opposition to his policies. Yet, the administration, remembering how Johnson had been tormented by protesters and had ended by rarely leaving the White House, was clearly worried.

In a speech to the nation, Nixon appealed for public backing as he outlined the Vietnamization plan. Addressing "the great silent majority of my fellow Americans," he said, "Let us understand: North Vietnam cannot defeat or humiliate the United States. Only Americans can do that."

The response to the address was favorable, but then a moritorium on November 15 drew more demonstrators than the month before. The gap between the "silent majority" and the antiwar demonstrators seemed to be growing.

The Mylai Massacre The demonstrations were fueled, in part, by the enormous publicity surrounding news of a war atrocity committed by American troops in Vietnam a year earlier and subsequently covered up by high-ranking officers. On March 16, 1968, a platoon from Charlie Company, 1st Battalion, 20th Infantry of the Americal Division, had entered a little hamlet known as **Mylai.** The hamlet was located in a heavily mined region in which the Vietcong had long operated, and several

NIXON AND THE WAR (1969-1973)

members of Charlie Company had been killed or maimed during the preceeding month. Although the troops received no opposing fire as they approached Mylai, their commander, Lieutenant **William Calley,**[4] ordered them to go in shooting. The killing went on for several hours, with numerous breaks in between, and when it was over between 200 and 300 Vietnamese civilians, mostly women and children, had been killed. The publicity surrounding the Mylai massacre was such that news accounts of the Communist atrocities in Hué (page 95), which were also just then coming to light, were completely overshadowed.

SECTION 1 REVIEW

1. **Vocabulary to Know** Walker Commission, Tet '69, Vietnamization, moritorium, Mylai

2. **People to Identify** Richard Nixon, Richard Daley, Hubert Humphrey, George Wallace, Henry Kissinger, Prince Norodom Sihanouk, Creighton Abrams, Melvin Laird, Spiro Agnew, William Calley

3. (a) Who won the Democratic presidential nomination in 1968? (b) What disagreement arose over the party's official position on Vietnam?

4. Why did Nixon order the bombing of Cambodia?

5. What did Nixon hope to achieve by his Vietnamization plan?

6. **Critical Thinking** Why do you think news of the Mylai massacre was such a shock to the American public?

2 THE UNITED STATES INVADES CAMBODIA

During the first year of Nixon's presidency nearly 10,000 Americans lost their lives in Vietnam, and the frustrations grew. For many Americans, a battle in May, 1969, pointed out the futility of the war. In the battle of **"Hamburger Hill,"** so named because of the many GI's ground up in the engagement, American forces captured Apbia mountain, near the Laotian border. A week later

---

[4.] Calley, an inept officer who was said not to be able even to read a map, was convicted in 1971 by a military court on a charge of premediated murder. Many saw him as a scapegoat, however, and the public outcry was such that Nixon reduced his life sentence to twenty years. Calley was released on good behavior three years later.

THE VIETNAM WAR

the hill was abandoned, as was common practice, because it held no military value and because success was measured not in terms of territory gained and held but by the number of enemy killed. There was wide criticism at home, however, when it was learned that the hill had been reoccupied by the North Vietnamese.

Life magazine aroused further public anguish when it published photographs of the 242 Americans slain in Vietnam in a single week. For these and other reasons, Washington instructed General Abrams to scale down the military effort. Nixon, however, would continue to look for an opportunity to take dramatic action to underscore his commitment to South Vietnam.

The Phoenix Program North Vietnam also found 1969 to be a tough year. It had to send large numbers of troops south to replace the Vietcong forces devastated during Tet, and by 1970 about two thirds of all Communist soldiers in South Vietnam were Northerners. Fighting far from home in terrain unfamiliar to them often proved difficult.

The remaining Vietcong were also suffering, but for an added reason. The controversial **Phoenix program,** first proposed by the Central Intelligence Agency in 1967 as a way to uproot Vietcong agents, had been reorganized. American specialists concentrated their efforts in training South Vietnamese military and civilian advisers in methods of penetrating the peasant population to gather information, identify Communist organizers, and then kill them.

By the estimates of **William Colby,** the CIA executive who ran the Phoenix program during the war, as many as 60,000 Vietcong agents were killed. Phoenix was, without question, a brutal program—indeed, antiwar activists branded it as mass murder. And outrages were committed. Villages were given monthly quotas, and innocent peasants were sometimes killed in the efforts to meet the assigned numbers. Payoffs were widespread too, with an estimated 70 percent of the Vietcong suspects paying bribes to win back their freedom. Still, many of the immediate goals of Phoenix were met. In many cases guerrilla bases were uncovered, and the Communist forces had no choice but to retreat to sanctuaries in Cambodia. Meanwhile, thousands of weary guerrillas surrendered to the Saigon regime or simply returned to their villages.

Vietnam by the End of 1969 As 1969 came to a close, then, many in the Nixon administration could claim that progress had been made in Vietnam. More than 100,000 Americans had been brought home, and there were plans to remove another 150,000 during 1970. For the Communists, weakened by the Phoenix program and by the devastating American bombing, victory remained a distant dream. Disheartened, they switched back to organizing small operations. It was at this time, however, that Nixon, looking for a way to shorten the war, decided upon a dramatic move. He would send American forces into Cambodia.

Chaos in Cambodia Ever since the start of the secret American bombing of Cambodia (page 111), the situation there had grown worse. To avoid the American bombs, the North Vietnamese had moved deeper into Cambodian territory. They had also begun to organize and train bands of Cambodian Communists known as the **Khmer Rouge.** A force of more than 10,000 Khmer Rouge was sent into Cambodia, and there were early signs that a brutal civil war was in the making.

On the other side, the Cambodian military was growing restless. Senior officers, along with the prime minister, General **Lon Nol,** wanted American help in evicting both the Khmer Rouge and the North Vietnamese from Cambodia. Plotting to seize power, they waited until January, 1970, when Sihanouk departed for the French Riviera for his yearly "cure" for obesity. In the prince's absence, the officers encouraged youths to riot against Vietnamese living in **Phnompenh,** Cambodia's capital, and many innocent Vietnamese civilians were slaughtered.

As chaos mounted in Cambodia, Sihanouk chose to remain overseas, fearing danger if he returned. He was in Moscow on March 18, 1970, when he received news that Lon Nol had overthrown him.

Sihanouk's ouster fanned the flames of disorder. Rival gangs rose up against one another, vigilantes continued to murder Vietnamese civilians, Communist troops pushed back the Cambodian army, and South Vietnamese units secretly penetrated Cambodian border areas. On April 14, 1970, Lon Nol, at the suggestion of American officials in Phnompenh, pleaded for help. Awaiting just such a signal, the United States prepared to step in.

The Invasion of Cambodia With Lon Nol on the verge of collapse, Nixon had the opportunity he had been waiting for. He moved secretly, first ordering that Lon Nol's forces be armed and trained by American advisers. Then, on April 22, 1970, two days after announcing to the nation that "we finally have in sight the just peace we are seeking," he dictated a memo to Kissinger calling for a "bold move" into Cambodia.

After administration figures debated several plans, the President decided to stage "the big play" by ordering American and

South Vietnamese units to attack sanctuaries all along the border region. On April 26, 1970, without informing Lon Nol, Nixon ordered American forces to prepare to invade Cambodia. Four days later, he announced in a televised address that the "incursion"[5] had begun. He explained that 20,000 troops had been ordered to destroy enemy supply depots and camps. This action, he claimed, would shorten the war and save American lives. Painting the situation as a challenge to America's global standing, he said, "If when the chips are down, the world's most powerful nation, the United States of America, acts like a pitiful helpless giant, the forces of totalitarianism and anarchy will threaten free nations and free institutions throughout the world."

Although Nixon had spoken of "the big play," he still imposed several restrictions on American commanders in the field. No troops could penetrate farther than 22 miles (35 kilometers) into Cambodia. The President also insisted that all United States forces leave Cambodia by June 30.

Unhappy with these restrictions, military commanders moved against the Cambodian sanctuaries and did the best they could. At the start of the American advance, most enemy forces had simply retreated deeper into Cambodia. Nevertheless, the invaders found huge amounts of supplies, and those that they could not remove in the time allotted were destroyed. Enough ammunition was found to supply Communist forces in South Vietnam for ten months, and there was enough rice to feed all enemy combat battalions for four months. Trucks, mines, grenades, rockets, individual weapons—all were destroyed in large quantities. Clearly the captured material would relieve the pressure on South Vietnam.

Still, the invasion was a disappointment. In the months that followed, North Vietnam was able to replace the lost supplies and simply shifted its operations to the northern provinces of South Vietnam. Meanwhile, the war had been expanded, and the United States now found itself responsible for propping up the shaky regime of Lon Nol.

Protests Against the Cambodian Invasion Domestic criticism of the President in this crucial moment was intense. Secretary of the Interior Walter Hickel voiced his objections and was later fired. More than 200 employees of the State Department signed a letter of protest. The Senate, for its part, voted overwhelmingly to repeal the Gulf of Tonkin Resolution (page 57).

[5.] Nixon used the word *incursion* (meaning "raid") rather than the broader, more ominous, *invasion*.

NIXON AND THE WAR (1969-1973)

VIETNAM FACT

A key objective of the Nixon administration during the Cambodian invasion was to find an almost legendary North Vietnamese headquarters thought to be near the South Vietnamese border. The President had suggested to the public that this "Pentagon East" directed all Communist operations in South Vietnam (even though the Defense Department had told him that it doubted whether such a heaquarters even existed). At one point Newsweek *magazine described the headquarters as "a fortified, reinforced concrete bunker with a staff of 2,300 organized into an elaborate series of bureaucratic sections." No such single headquarters was ever found, and most military observers doubted that one had ever existed.*

College and university campuses were the scene of many demonstrations, some of which turned violent. The most noteworthy incident took place at **Kent State** University, in Ohio. Kent State was an unlikely campus for a violent demonstration. Its student body was from working-class families, and up to now there had been little antiwar sentiment on the basically conservative campus. Following a peaceful protest against the invasion, however, spontaneous riots had broken out, and students had attacked and burned the reserve officers training building. Governor James Rhodes, threatening to "eradicate" the troublemakers, declared martial law and ordered national guardsmen onto the campus with loaded rifles.

On May 4, 1970, the guardsmen watched as students assembled peacefully but in defiance of the martial law. After they refused to disperse, some students hurled rocks at guard members and, even after tear gas was fired at them, continued to do so. Then, without warning, the nervous guardsmen aimed their rifles and began shooting. Four youths were killed—two demonstrators and two passers-by—and ten others were wounded.[6]

[6.] Violence flared three days later at the University of Buffalo where police wounded four protesting students. On May 14, state police killed two students on the campus of Jackson State College, in Mississippi.

THE VIETNAM WAR

The Kent State killings ignited nationwide protests. More than 400 colleges and universities shut down as students organized strikes, and at 26 schools a state of emergency was declared and the National Guard called in. On May 9 over 100,000 people marched on Washington to demand an end to the war. During the Washington demonstration, Nixon, who had earlier been quoted as calling the students "bums blowing up campuses," mingled with a late-night crowd of young dissidents at the Lincoln Memorial. Making awkward conversation, he engaged in a rambling monologue about sports before returning to the White House.

Two Camps There were increasing signs that the Vietnam War was dividing the nation. In New York City 100,000 construction workers marched in an angry demonstration of support for the President's policies. Meanwhile, a new song by a popular folk-rock group—Crosby, Stills, Nash, and Young—was climbing the charts. Entitled "Four Dead in Ohio," it contained the lyrics, "Soldiers are gunning us down." America, it appeared, had been divided in two camps: "us" and "them."

Restored to his natural combativeness soon after his visit to the Lincoln Memorial, Nixon went on the attack. Of his congressional critics, he advised his staff, "Don't worry about divisiveness. Having drawn the sword, don't take it out. Stick it in hard. Hit 'em in the gut." He sent Spiro Agnew out onto the campaign trail, where the Vice President attacked the protesters in angry speeches. (The Republicans would make minor gains in the November congressional elections.) Agnew also attacked the findings of a special commission named by the President to study the tense domestic situation. The commission, headed by former Pennsylvania governor William Scranton, found the split in American society "as deep as any since the Civil War" and argued that "nothing is more important than an end to the war."

The White House felt the split too. One of Nixon's chief aides, Chuck Colson, recalled, "Within the iron gates of the White House, quite unknowingly, a siege mentality was setting in. It was now 'us' against 'them.' Gradually, as we drew the circle closer around us, the ranks of 'them' began to swell."

As the gap widened, Nixon had a former army intelligence officer named Tom Huston draw up a plan that suggested ways of secretly gaining information about his critics, including burglary. Huston warned that such activity was probably illegal, but Nixon ordered him to go ahead anyway. In defense of the **Huston Plan** and other shady activities, Nixon would say, "When the President does it, that means it is not illegal."

SECTION 2 REVIEW

1. **Vocabulary to Know** "Hamburger Hill," Phoenix program, Khmer Rouge, Phnompenh, Kent State, Huston Plan

2. **People to Identify** William Colby, Lon Nol

3. What success did the Phoenix program have?

4. (a) Why did Nixon order the invasion of Cambodia? (b) What were the results of the operation?

5. What effect did the Kent State tragedy have on the rest of the nation?

6. **Critical Thinking** Why do you think the Cambodian invasion provoked such a heated reaction at home?

3 THE WAR GRINDS ON

Early in 1970, as the formal Paris peace talks droned on, Henry Kissinger met in secret in a suburb of the French capital with **Le Duc Tho.** A leading North Vietnamese official, Le Duc Tho had helped found the Indochinese Communist Party, had been the top Vietminh leader in southern Vietnam during the war against the French, and had later organized resistance in that region to the United States. Kissinger chose to talk secretly with him because he wanted to cut out the State Department from the negotiations and because, too, he wanted to distance himself from the demands of the South Vietnamese government. In Le Duc Tho, however, he found a tough, almost fanatical adversary who saw negotiations simply as another means of warfare and a process that could go on forever until his goals were met. Not for three years would a peace treaty be signed.

A Standstill Cease-fire Nixon was faced with a dilemna. American troops continued to be brought home, but now the fighting had spread into Cambodia. Even Laos was affected, as the North Vietnamese stepped up their activity in that country. The war, it was apparent, had spread to all of Indochina, and more was at stake than ever before.

Partially to reassure his critics at home and partially because he lacked maneuvering room to do much of anything else, Nixon on October 7, 1970, announced a **standstill cease-fire** plan.

According to this idea, both sides would stop fighting and remain where they were, while an international conference would meet to draw up a settlement. Nixon also promised to bring home another 90,000 Americans by the following spring.

Congress greeted the standstill cease-fire plan warmly, and antiwar critics on Capitol Hill signed a resolution of praise. But the North Vietnamese rejected the truce plan, calling first for Communist representation in a coalition government in Saigon. (This was really another way of insisting on President Thieu's resignation.) A few days later, Nixon was again calling for the withdrawal of North Vietnamese troops from the South—the original American position all along. Many observers suspected that the truce plan was only intended as a means of gaining voter support in the upcoming American congressional elections (page 120).

The Invasion of Laos The presidential elections of 1972 were on the mind of administration officials too. Assuming that the North Vietnamese were planning on a big offensive to influence those elections, military commanders in Saigon decided on a surprise move to block the expected influx of troops and supplies from the North. They would cut the Ho Chi Minh Trail by advancing into Laos.

A congressional amendment passed in 1970 after the Cambodian incursion banned the use of American ground troops in Cambodia or Laos. The invasion of Laos, as a result, would have to be carried out by South Vietnamese forces with American air support. It would be the first real test of Vietnamization.

The invasion plans were poorly conceived. American planners had called for an invading army of 60,000 men, but the South Vietnamese assigned an inexperienced army of only half that size. Thieu instructed his forces to halt their advance, moreover, if they suffered more than 3,000 casualties—hardly fighting orders. Their target, the Laotian town of Tchepone was, finally, within easy firing range of North Vietnamese units in the area.

The South Vietnamese began their cautious advance into Laos on February 8, 1971. They captured Tchepone, which American bombers had reduced to rubble, but once they had reached the worthless target, they were fired upon by North Vietnamese artillery. A pull-back soon turned into a wild, uncontrolled retreat. Newspapers and television cameras captured images of panicked ARVN soldiers crowding onto American helicopters that had been sent in to remove the wounded. Some soldiers even dangled from the landing gear of the departing choppers.

NIXON AND THE WAR (1969-1973)

Discouragement In a televised speech a few weeks after the Laos disaster, Nixon announced that Vietnamization had "succeeded." In private, however, he recognized what was plain for all to see: that the South Vietnamese army simply was not prepared to take over the fighting. For too long it had been led by cautious, incompetent officers whose promotions depended on their loyalty to Thieu, not to their performances on the battlefield. (Indeed, battlefield success was a political handicap, for an officer might then be viewed as overly ambitious and a potential threat to those in power.)

The Laotian setback was a major disappointment to Saigon. A wave of nervousness swept the nation as a result of the army's poor showing. There was growing fear that the continuing withdrawal of the Americans would leave the country to the mercies of the North Vietnamese. Meanwhile, in Washington 30,000 demonstrators arrived in the nation's capital, threatening to "shut the government down." Mobs roamed the streets, leading to ugly riots and the arrests of some 12,000 people, many of whom were held without being charged of any specific offense.

Problems of Morale Throughout most of the war, Americans in Vietnam had fought well, despite the miserable conditions they faced. Now, however, military leaders were increasingly faced with a new problem—that of morale.

There were many explanations for the decline in morale. With the number of American troops in Vietnam now being reduced, for one thing, the goal of most soldiers was to avoid injury or death and to finish their tours of duty safely. No one wanted to be the last to die in a cause that had clearly lost its meaning. "If Nixon is going to withdraw," said one soldier, "then let's all go home now." There were fewer offensive operations, fewer patrols, as the United States army fell into a defensive posture.

Many soldiers had also been influenced by antiwar protests at home. At first, the troops had resented the protesters, especially students who were exempt from the draft. But gradually, men in the field began decorating their helmets and uniforms with peace symbols. Soon, they were using the two-finger peace sign as a means of saluting.

The general rebellion at home against authority had its effect in Vietnam as well. After the wide publicity surrounding the Mylai massacre, many GI's suspected their commanders of covering up other atrocities. Orders were questioned or disobeyed, and in some cases troops refused to fight. There were even a growing number of incidents called **fragging**—the attempted murder of superior officers with fragmentation grenades.[7] In 1970 as many as 45 officers lost their lives in fragging attacks.

Military officers were frustrated too. Many felt betrayed by the policy of withdrawal. In the words of one major, "We won the war, that's what kills us. We fought the North Vietnamese to a standstill and bolstered the South Vietnamese army and government. But we can't persuade anybody of that." A number of officers resigned. Others became cynical and only put in their time as a means of advancing their careers. They often had less combat exposure than the troops they led, a fact that led to smoldering resentment.

Many troops, seeking an escape from the war, turned to drugs. Marijuana was widely available and cost next to nothing. According to a 1971 official estimate, nearly 60 percent of the American soldiers in Vietnam were marijuana users. Even more troublesome was the presence of heroin. The source was the region stretching across northern Laos, Burma, and Thailand, known as the "Golden Triangle." Corrupt South Vietnamese officers and government officials controlled the flow of heroin into Saigon, though they were hardly alone. American pilots also took part in smuggling the addictive drug, and in one embarrassing incident the pilot of Ambassador Ellsworth Bunker was arrested with $8 million worth of heroin in his plane. By 1971 a shocking one third of the American troops in Vietnam had experimented with heroin or opium. In that year, four times as many soldiers required treatment for serious drug abuse as did those undergoing hospital treatment for combat wounds.

It cannot be surprising that racial frustrations grew worse as the war went on, reflecting the heated atmosphere at home. Black servicemen became more outspoken in denouncing discrimination in the military, and as tension mounted, racial violence broke out (though rarely when units were in the field). To reduce friction, the military set up grievance sessions and civil rights committees to hear and discuss racial complaints. Restrictions were also lifted against modified Afro haircuts and against elaborate handshakes called "daps." Still, dissatisfaction among black servicemen remained high.

A final problem had to do with the nature of the troops themselves. During World War II, the average age of American soldiers was 26; in Vietnam the average age was 19. In addition to being older and more mature, World War II troops fought for no

---

[7] Fragmentation grenades leave no fingerprints and are, therefore, a convenient murder weapon. Fragging became a general term for all attacks on fellow servicemen with grenades, rifles, or knives.

longer than six to eight weeks at a time; troops in Vietnam were, in a sense, always on the firing line since no territory could be considered "safe." This combination—younger troops and the long periods of stress—resulted in a disillusioned fighting force, an army that by the early 1970's some observers were calling a shambles. "A lot of our buddies got killed here but they died for nothing," summed up one GI. "Our morale, man, it's so low you can't see it."

The Pentagon Papers By early 1971, Nixon's standing in the public opinion polls had slipped drastically. Just 34 percent of those polled supported his handling of the war. Nixon was also harmed by the publication in *The New York Times,* beginning in June, 1971, of excerpts from the so-called **Pentagon Papers.** This was a secret study of the role of the United States in Vietnam that had been commissioned in 1967 by Robert McNamara. It had been given to the *Times* by **Daniel Ellsberg,** who had worked on the report.

For many observers, the huge collection of confidential government memos offered proof that the American public had been continually deceived about the real situation in Vietnam. Nixon and Kissinger were appalled. They feared that the public's faith in administration policies would continue to fall. They also felt that the publication of secret information would harm national security.

Nixon had the government sue to stop the *Times* from publishing further extracts. The case quickly went to the Supreme Court, but the justices refused to intervene and allowed the papers to be printed.

The Plumbers Meanwhile, the President looked for new ways to strike back at his opponents. He formed a secret special unit, jokingly known as the **plumbers** since its job was to stop "leaks" of information to the press. E. Howard Hunt, a former CIA agent, and G. Gordon Liddy, once with the FBI, reported to Nixon's special counsel, Charles Colson. Their first assignment, to find some way to ruin Daniel Ellsberg's reputation, ended in failure. Breaking into the Los Angeles office of Ellsberg's psychiatrist, the plumbers found nothing of interest.[8]

Another activity of the plumbers was to draw up an "enemies list" of administration opponents. Continually updated, the 200-name list included such establishment figures as the presidents

---

[8.] Hunt and other top Nixon aides—including John Ehrlichman, the President's assistant for domestic affairs—would later be convicted for this break-in and sent to jail.

of Yale, the Harvard Law School, the World Bank, and the Ford Foundation; United States senators Edward Kennedy, Walter Mondale, and Edmund Muskie; political activists Jane Fonda, Dick Gregory, and Bella Abzug; and, incredibly, such non-political figures as actors Steve McQueen and Gregory Peck, and football star Joe Namath. The largest number of "enemies," however—57 in all—were journalists and other media figures.

The plumbers also undertook a campaign to try and blame the Democrats for the Vietnam War. Forged documents tying President Kennedy directly to the plot to assassinate Ngo Dinh Diem were planted in the press. Finally, in an effort to gain information, the plumbers broke into the Democratic National Headquarters in the Watergate complex in Washington, D.C. The Watergate scandal, which would lead to Nixon's resignation in 1974, thus had its beginning in the Vietnam War.

Détente It was during these months that Nixon was moving ahead with the major diplomatic moves that he had contemplated at the beginning of his presidency. In July, 1971, Kissinger secretly flew to China for a meeting with Zhou Enlai, now that nation's premier. A few days after the visit, Nixon surprised the world by announcing that he had accepted an invitation to visit China. To describe his new policy, which he said would reduce tensions and bring peace to the world, he used the word **détente** (from the French, meaning "to ease or relax").

On February 2, 1972, the President flew to China, and the work of bringing the relations of the two countries back to normal was begun. A few months later, Nixon followed up his dramatic visit with a summit conference in Moscow with **Leonid Brezhnev,** the Soviet premier. A number of important agreements were signed, including a pledge to slow down the nuclear arms race.

The Communist Offensive of 1972 There were not many Americans left in South Vietnam by 1972. Of the 70,000 troops remaining, only 6,000 were combat troops—and their activities were restricted. As a result, Hanoi earmarked the year as a good time to test the strength of the Saigon government's army. That army had more than a million men under arms, but even so it was stretched thin, with most troops holding defensive positions. By defeating the South Vietnamese, the Communists hoped to prove that Vietnamization was a failure and that the United States should agree to a settlement in Paris on their terms. They also assumed that since it was a presidential election year in the United States, the Americans would not re-introduce troops into Vietnam.

NIXON AND THE WAR (1969-1973)

More than 120,000 North Vietnamese troops, supported by Vietcong guerrillas, attacked locations throughout South Vietnam on March 30, 1972. Sweeping across the northern part of the country, and backed for the first time by long-range heavy artillery, they captured the provincial capital of Quangtri on May 1 and held it through the summer. They also proved to be strong in the central highlands and near the Cambodian border. To meet the Communist threat, Thieu ordered several big battalions in the Mekong Delta to move north. Once they did, Communist forces rushed into the densely populated region, seizing more than a hundred government posts.

A day after the Communist attacks began, Nixon ordered American aircraft to start massive raids against the North. For the first time, targets once off-limit in the Hanoi area were hit, and Haiphong harbor was mined.

The Communists were in a quandary. Even though they made significant gains in their latest offensive, particularly in the Mekong Delta, they had lost as many as 50,000 dead. Moreover, they had not been able to defeat the South Vietnamese. The American air attacks, which had not brought the expected protests from the Soviet Union, were taking their toll. Finally, as Election Day neared in the United States, it appeared that Nixon was headed for a landslide victory over the Democratic nominee, **George McGovern,** an antiwar senator from South Dakota. For these reasons, the North Vietnamese decided to call off the attacks and compromise with the Americans. For the time being, they would not insist on Thieu's removal. An agreement suddenly seemed near.

SECTION 3 REVIEW

1. **Vocabulary to Know** standstill cease-fire, fragging, Pentagon Papers, plumbers, détente

2. **People to Identify** Le Duc Tho, Daniel Ellsberg, Leonid Brezhnev, George McGovern

3. What were the results of the South Vietnamese invasion of Laos?

4. What morale problems did the United States military face?

5. **Critical Thinking** What connection is there between the Vietnam War and the Watergate affair?

CHAPTER 6 REVIEW

Vocabulary and People

Spiro Agnew
Leonid Brezhnev
William Calley
William Colby
Richard Daley
détente
Daniel Ellsberg
fragging
"Hamburger Hill"
Hubert Humphrey
Huston Plan
Kent State
Khmer Rouge
Henry Kissinger
Melvin Laird
George McGovern

Lon Nol
moritorium
Mylai
Richard Nixon
Pentagon Papers
Phoenix program
Phnompenh
plumbers
Prince Norodom Sihanouk
standstill cease-fire
Tet '69
Le Duc Tho
Vietnamization
Walker Commission
George Wallace

Identification

Identify the following people. Name the country with which each was connected and tell why that person was important.

1. Leonid Brezhnev

2. Henry Kissinger

3. Lon Nol

4. Prince Norodom Sihanouk

5. Le Duc Tho

Reviewing the Main Ideas

1. How did the national debate over Vietnam affect the Democratic Party and the election of 1968?

2. In an effort to shorten the war, how did Nixon end by widening it?

NIXON AND THE WAR (1969-1973)

3. What problems did Nixon's Vietnamization plan encounter?

4. What was the chief difference dividing the two sides at the Paris peace talks?

5. (a) How strong was the American position in Vietnam by 1972? (b) How strong were the Communists?

Critical Thinking

Curtis LeMay, former Air Force Chief of Staff and the running mate of George Wallace in the 1968 presidential race, made the following comments at a press conference during the campaign. Read LeMay's words and then answer the questions that follow:

> We seem to have a phobia [great fear] about nuclear weapons. The smart thing to do when you're in a war ...[is] get in with both feet and get it over with as soon as you can.... Use the force that's necessary. Maybe use a little more to make sure it's enough to stop the fighting as soon as possible.... I think there are many times when it would be most efficient to use nuclear weapons.

1. (a) What was LeMay's view of the use of nuclear weapons? (b) What advantages did he believe nuclear weapons offer?

2. What might account for the "phobia" Americans have about nuclear weapons?

3. Compare LeMay's view with that of Lady Bird Johnson (page 89). With which do you agree? Why?

4. Do research to find out the effect LeMay's statement had on Wallace's election chances.

Air Force sentry, Danang Air Base.

CHAPTER SEVEN

WITHDRAWAL AND AFTERMATH

(1973 TO THE PRESENT)

AFTER NEARLY A DECADE OF INTENSE AND frustrating involvement in Vietnam, the last American troops left that war-ravaged country in 1973. The cease-fire, under which the terms of the American withdrawal were stated, did not last long however. Two years later, when the North Vietnamese launched a major offensive, South Vietnam's forces collapsed with stunning speed. Vietnam was reunified under a Communist government, and the United States was left to ponder and debate what it had learned.

In this chapter you will learn the fate of Vietnam and its neighboring countries in the years since the American withdrawal. As you read, look for answers to the following questions:

1. **What happened to South Vietnam after the United States withdrawal?**
2. **What has happened to Southeast Asia in recent years?**

1 THE UNITED STATES WITHDRAWAL LEADS TO A COMMUNIST VICTORY

American withdrawal from Vietnam did not come easily. Nixon's Vietnamization plan continued to bring troops home, but a peace settlement, which in the fall of 1972 seemed so near, proved hard to reach.

A North Vietnamese Offer On October 8, 1972, Le Duc Tho and Henry Kissinger met again in Paris. The North Vietnamese delegate proposed a cease-fire, the withdrawal of American troops, and the formation of a coalition government which would make plans for elections. These arrangements, in theory, would lead to a peaceful end to the war. Until then, Communist and South Vietnamese troops would hold the areas they occupied at the time of the agreement.

Kissinger, desperate for an agreement before the American presidential elections in early November, was overjoyed. He urged President Thieu to seize as much territory as possible, and had the Pentagon speed delivery of some $2 billion in arms to bolster the South Vietnamese. Instead of dismantling its bases, furthermore, the United States simply transferred title to the South Vietnamese. Nixon, meanwhile, gave Thieu "absolute assurances" that any North Vietnamese violation of the agreement would be met with "swift and severe retaliatory action," and he ordered the Joint Chiefs to begin planning for such an event.

Thieu, however, was not so sure. He mistrusted any settlement that would allow the North Vietnamese to remain on his soil. He also suspected that the United States was about to abandon him. To keep Thieu in line, Nixon threatened to cut off all American aid to South Vietnam. Yet Nixon, too, was not convinced that the North Vietnamese offer was a good one. He constantly changed his mind during the days and weeks that followed, wanting an agreement but fearing that a Communist take-over might be the result.

"Peace Is at Hand" To encourage a settlement, Kissinger spoke at his first public press conference ever on October 24. "We believe that peace is at hand," he dramatically stated. "We believe that an agreement is within sight." The American public, amidst general relief and rejoicing, took this statement to mean that the Vietnam War was over. The presidential election was held, with Nixon scoring a triumphant victory over McGovern. The President carried all but one state, winning 60 percent of the popular

WITHDRAWAL AND AFTERMATH (1973 TO THE PRESENT)

vote. The Paris talks, however, were coming apart. Because of disagreements over amendments to the draft agreement proposed by the South Vietnamese, Le Duc Tho called off the talks and left Paris in mid-December.

The suspension of the talks, when an agreement had seemed so near, left Nixon frustrated and furious. He sent a harsh message to the North Vietnamese, giving them 72 hours to start talking "seriously"—or else. At the same time, he ordered preparations for massive raids on Hanoi and Haiphong. To Admiral Thomas Moorer, Chairman of the Joint Chiefs of Staff, he said, "This is your chance to use military power to win this war, and if you don't, I'll hold you responsible."

The Christmas Bombings When time had run out, Nixon gave the signal for the bombing to begin. Starting on December 18, more than 3,000 sorties were flown against the heavily populated area around Hanoi and Haiphong. Fifty thousand tons of bombs were dropped in the controversial raids, which went on for twelve days. Known as the **Christmas bombings** (even though no aircraft actually flew on Christmas Day), the attacks devastated their military targets. Airfields, roads, and rail lines were knocked out, as was 80 percent of the country's electrical power production. More tonnage was dropped on North Vietnam than during the entire period from 1969 to 1971.

Civilian targets were avoided and the official loss of life, placed by the North Vietnamese government at 1,318 in Hanoi and 305 in Haiphong, was amazingly low. Still, in spite of the extreme caution to avoid civilian targets, American pilots could not avoid killing innocent citizens and destroying nonmilitary targets. In a highly publicized incident, a B-52 missed its target by 1,000 meters and hit **Bach Mai,** the largest hospital in Hanoi. Twenty-eight people were killed, bringing worldwide condemnation.

Peace Settlement The Christmas bombings demonstrated to Thieu that the United States would make good on its promise to punish the North Vietnamese if they violated any settlement. They also achieved their desired purpose in getting the North Vietnamese back to the bargaining table.

On January, 8, 1973, Kissinger and Le Duc Tho resumed their discussions and quickly reached an agreement. The **Paris peace settlement** was virtually the same as the draft offered in October: the chief point stipulated that both the North Vietnamese and South Vietnamese forces would remain on the territory each occupied. With the formal signing ceremony on January 27, 1973,

Nixon could say, "We have finally achieved peace with honor."[1] With so many North Vietnamese troops in South Vietnam, however, it was clearly just a matter of time before the fighting broke out again.

Prisoners of War Under the Paris agreement, all American prisoners of war (POW's) held in North Vietnam were to be released. Some 9,000 American airplanes and helicopters had been lost since 1961 in Indochina, and 2,000 pilots and crew members had been killed. Nearly 600 Americans had been held captive in the North, often in cruel circumstances. Many were kept in solitary cells in the **Hanoi Hilton** and other jails, and they were frequently tortured.

In February, 1973, the first POW's began arriving home. At a White House reception on May 24, 1973, President Nixon greeted many of them, including Everett Alvarez, the longest-held prisoner (page 57). The return of the POW's marked the end of the war for most Americans.

A Weakened Nixon While the POW's were being released, the government of Nguyen Van Thieu nervously eyed the roughly 150,000 North Vietnamese troops who had been allowed to stay in place in South Vietnam. Thieu's army, equipped with the latest American weapons, controlled most of South Vietnam's territory and population. But already there were ominous signs. Congress, eager to reclaim a role in directing American foreign policy, passed a bill on June 4, 1973, that blocked funds for any United States military activity in Indochina. Nixon, who previously had assured Thieu that "We will respond with full force should the settlement be violated by North Vietnam," was powerless to stop the congressional action. The Watergate affair was destroying his presidency, and Congress had the upper hand.

It is doubtful, moreover, that the American public, sick to death of Vietnam, would have supported any proposal to back Thieu directly. Reflecting the public's view, Congress passed the **War Powers Act** late in 1973, overriding Nixon's veto. The legislation, a response to the secret, unilateral actions of Presidents during the Vietnam War, requires the Chief Executive to inform Congress within 48 hours of the deployment of American military forces abroad. The troops must be withdrawn if, within 60 days, Congress does not approve the deployment.

---

[1] On that same day, Defense Secretary Laird announced the end of the military draft in America.

WITHDRAWAL AND AFTERMATH (1973 TO THE PRESENT)

Problems Facing Thieu Thieu had other worries also. During the war years, millions of refugees had swollen South Vietnam's cities.[2] There they joined scores of people who were searching for work. Many of the new urban dwellers had depended on the Americans and the booming wartime economy for a living. It is estimated that perhaps 2 million of South Vietnam's 17 million people relied on the Americans for their livelihood.

With the departure of the United States, however, many jobs vanished and unemployment became a major headache. At the same time, inflation was climbing, due in part to the Arab oil embargo imposed following the 1973 Middle East war. With soaring prices, most soldiers were not receiving enough money to support their families, and army morale suffered. Corruption too was growing unchecked. Army officers looted payrolls by keeping on the rosters the names of dead and deserted soldiers so they could pocket the pay. Pilots actually demanded bribes before flying missions in support of ground troops. Meanwhile the Buddhists, long quiet, were again demonstrating against the government. Even the Catholics, the government's chief core of support, organized an anti-corruption campaign, aimed chiefly at Thieu himself.

At the same time, the Communists were quietly strengthening their forces and making plans for the coming struggle. They began moving tanks, trucks, and armored vehicles south over newly built roads, and even constructed a pipeline so that their forces would have adequate supplies of petroleum. They watched with deep interest, too, as Congress in 1974 cut a $1 billion appropriation in military aid to South Vietnam to $700 million. The cut was made shortly after Richard Nixon, facing certain impeachment, resigned from office. His successor, **Gerald Ford**, promised that he would support Thieu, but the new President's options appeared limited.

The Final Communist Offensive By early 1975, the North Vietnamese were divided between those eager to launch a big drive against Saigon and those taking a more cautious approach. A decision was made to attack Phuoc Long, a mountainous province just sixty miles north of Saigon, and see what happened. To the Communists' surprise, they easily captured the provincial capital of Phuoc Binh, and went on to take the entire province. In so doing, they noted that the Americans had virtually ignored the situation. The South Vietnamese, it was now obvious, could no

---

[2.] Between 1955 and 1970, for example, Saigon's population had swelled from 300,000 to 3,000,000.

THE VIETNAM WAR

longer call on the devastating air power formally provided by the United States. Encouraged, the North Vietnamese looked for another target and decided on the town of Banmethuot, in the central highlands. Again, they scored an easy victory.

The Convoy of Tears With the central highlands in danger, Thieu made a fateful decision: he chose to withdraw government forces from the central highlands in order to protect Saigon. The general in charge of the withdrawal immediately flew out of the area, leaving arrangements in the hands of an officer with little command experience. Troops began to retreat in disorder, setting off a general panic. Hundreds of thousands of refugees fled with the soldiers, choking the route of escape.

The torrent of refugees, heading in terror toward the coast, was known as the **convoy of tears**. As many as 30,000 people were killed as the North Vietnamese shelled the highway on which the soldiers and refugees fled. Some civilians were shot by desperate, rampaging ARVN soldiers or were simply trampled to death by mobs of people out of control.

The Fall of Danang Meanwhile, another huge convoy of trucks and cars was moving south along the coast. The pull-back of troops from the Quangtri area near the North Vietnamese border had unleashed another chaotic retreat. By late March, more than a million men, women, and children were heading toward Danang. Many were panic-stricken residents of Hué who remembered the Communist atrocities committed during the Tet offensive of 1968. The evacuation of the historic capital of Hué, captured from the Communists at such heavy cost in 1968, was a severe blow to the nation's morale.

Danang, the base of the first American combat troops in South Vietnam, had long been a symbol of American military power. Now it was jammed with desperate refugees and soldiers, all determined to make their way farther south. With Communist forces approaching Danang, however, there were mass scenes of terror and chaos. Tens of thousands of people fought to make room for themselves on boats or in airplanes.

On March 30, 1975, Danang fell to the Communists. South Vietnam had been cut in two, and about half its army had been lost without putting up any resistance. Key bases, such as Camranh Bay, had been abandoned before enemy troops even arrived in the area.

The View from America Each night, television newscasts showed the heartrending, chaotic scenes of Vietnam's collapse. Some Americans, who had always emphasized the corruption and inefficiency of the South Vietnamese government, welcomed what promised to be a speedy end of the Saigon regime. Others were shocked that an ally, which the United States had promised to protect and support, was being allowed to collapse so quickly. For Americans who had lost family members in combat, the loss of Vietnam was particularly hard to understand.

With the situation daily becoming more desperate, President Thieu requested a big increase in military and economic aid to his country. Gerald Ford, arguing that the amount requested was "relatively small compared to the $150 billion that we spent," urged passage of the emergency appropriation. Congress, concerned with problems in the domestic economy and tired of having to bail out the Saigon regime, refused. Members of Congress pointed out that the South Vietnamese had left behind more equipment in the northern provinces than could be purchased with the additional funds. Congress eventually approved $300 million in "humanitarian" aid, but no more. Its action seemed to reflect the will of the American people.

For Thieu, Congress's refusal was a betrayal. The secret promises made a few years earlier by Nixon, it now turned out, would not be kept: there would be no more military aid, no return of the B-52's. This knowledge seems to have paralyzed Thieu, and for many days he issued no orders. Without his leadership, the government ground to a halt, since no one of talent or initiative had been trusted enough to be given a position of authority.

The Move Toward Saigon Astonished by their successes, the Communists now made plans to attack Saigon as quickly as possible. They wanted to take advantage of the government forces' disorder; they also wanted to make their final move before the rainy season started in May.

In Saigon the American ambassador, **Graham Martin,** faced an agonizing situation. Some 6,000 Americans remained in the city, along with more than 200,000 Vietnamese who had worked for American agencies and were thought to be on North Vietnamese execution lists. Martin was urged to order their immediate departure, but he feared that if he did so he would start a panic. He refused to order a rescue operation, choosing to believe that Saigon could be held.

Resistance to the onrushing Communists was sporadic. Only at Xuanloc, the last defense line 35 miles northeast of Saigon, did South Vietnamese forces fight well. After a two-week battle, however, Xuanloc was in ruins and the defenders' ammunition was gone. Now there was nothing to stop the North Vietnamese from entering Saigon.

As the Communists approached, Saigon buzzed with rumors

of plots against Thieu. The President resigned on April 21, vowing to stay on and fight. "I resign, but I do not desert," he vowed. Four days later Thieu fled Saigon, carrying with him fifteen tons of baggage in which he had reportedly stashed millions of dollars in gold. Eventually he settled in Great Britain.

Nguyen Cao Ky, former premier and vice president of South Vietnam, at first talked tough too, promising to lead a defense of the city. Soon he commandeered a helicopter and flew it to the deck of the *USS Midway* lying off the coast.

The Fall of Saigon Two days before Thieu's departure, President Ford accepted what was now inevitable. The war was finished, he said, "as far as America is concerned. Today, Americans can regain the sense of pride that existed before Vietnam. But it cannot be achieved by re-fighting a war."

With Thieu gone, General Duoung Van Minh, who had helped overthrow Diem in 1963, was made head of state. The next day, on April 29, the Communists began rocketing the Saigon airport. By then, a fleet of helicopters was removing the last Americans from the city. Many of the choppers had to land on helicopter pads atop the United States embassy itself. The embassy compound was the scene of disorder and chaos as tens of thousands of people fought to find places on the evacuation flights. Mobs of people began scaling the embassy's ten-foot walls, and the defending marines had to use tear gas to hold the surging people back. By the morning of April 30, the last marines had left the embassy and the evacuation was complete. In the final days of April, more than 1,000 Americans and 6,000 Vietnamese had reached the safety of aircraft carriers waiting off shore.

On the morning of April 30, 1975, a North Vietnamese armored column was inside Saigon, heading through deserted streets towards the presidential place. The first North Vietnamese officer to reach the palace was Colonel Bui Tin. Upon accepting Minh's surrender, Bui Tin pulled out a short speech. "Between Vietnamese there are no victors and no vanquished," he read. "Only the Americans have been beaten. If you are patriots, consider this a moment of joy. The war for our country is over." After decades of fighting, Vietnam was a single nation under a Communist government.

SECTION 1 REVIEW

1. **Vocabulary to Know** Christmas bombings, Bach Mai, Paris peace settlement, Hanoi Hilton, War Powers Act, convoy of tears

WITHDRAWAL AND AFTERMATH (1973 TO THE PRESENT)

2. **People to Identify** Gerald Ford, Graham Martin

3. Why did Nixon order the Christmas bombings?

4. What part of the Paris peace settlement was sure to cause problems for South Vietnam?

5. What decision by Thieu helped bring on the final collapse?

6. **Critical Thinking** Was Congress justifying in refusing to provide Thieu with more aid as Communist troops closed in on Saigon? Explain your answer.

2 SOUTHEAST ASIA REMAINS A REGION OF TURMOIL AND CONFUSION

One of the reasons for American involvement in Southeast Asia was belief in the domino theory, the assumption that the entire region would collapse if the Communists won in Vietnam. With the victory of North Vietnam, two dominoes did topple—Laos and Cambodia. Outside of Indochina, however, the dominoes did *not* fall. In the years since 1975 most of the non-Communist countries of Southeast Asia have prospered and have watched, along with the rest of the world, as Vietnam has sunk deeper into disorder and poverty.

Communist Take-Over in Laos Once the focal point of President Kennedy's attention (page 39), Laos had ended by being a sideshow to the main events of the Vietnam War. The settlement of 1962 had set up a neutralist government, but outsiders had continued to wage war on Laotian soil. North Vietnamese infiltration routes into South Vietnam crossed over Laotian territory. Meanwhile, the North Vietnamese helped organize and train Laotian Communists, known as the **Pathet Lao.**

To confront the Communist activity, the United States waged a secret war in Laos from 1962 to 1972. Indeed, when the American bombing of North Vietnam was halted in 1968, Laos became the primary target. More than two million tons of bombs were dropped there by 1973. At the same time, the United States sponsored an army of its own. Comprised mainly of Hmong or Meo tribesmen, this force waged guerrilla warfare against North Vietnamese troops moving south along the Ho Chi Minh Trail.

The withdrawal of the United States from South Vietnam left

the anti-Communist forces of Laos without any chance of victory. An agreement in February, 1973, created a new government dominated by the Pathet Lao. Then, in 1975, soon after the fall of Saigon, the Pathet Lao took over. In the years since then, Laos has virtually become a province of Vietnam.

The Agony of Cambodia Events in Vietnam mirrored those in Cambodia. As North Vietnamese units closed in on Saigon, the Cambodian Communists tightened the noose around Phnompenh. There, the inept Lon Nol offered little resistance. His forces had been almost totally dependent on American air power, but in August, 1973, Congress had ordered all bombing in Cambodia halted.[3] On April 17, 1975, the Cambodian capital fell to the Khmer Rouge, days after Lon Nol had fled to Hawaii in exile.

In five years of fighting, as many as 500,000 Cambodians had been killed or wounded, most by American bombs. The suffering of the Cambodian people was, sadly, not over. Now they found themselves in the grips of the fanatical leader of the Khmer Rouge, **Pol Pot.**

In his youth, Pol Pot had studied in Paris. There he had picked up the idea of creating an ideal, agrarian state. Later, he had been influenced by a concept of Mao Zedong's, that of never-ending revolution. Now, in an effort to rebuild Cambodia from the "Year Zero," the ruthless Pol Pot seized the opportunity to put his ideas into effect—with devastating results.

Within hours of entering Phnompenh, the Khmer Rouge ordered the city emptied. The residents of all other towns and cities in Cambodia were also forced to leave their homes. Some observers thought that Pol Pot's aim was to mobilize workers for the rice harvest. Others assumed that he wanted to ease the economic pressure on the refugee-swollen cities. Later the truth was revealed. The Khmer Rouge had, in effect, declared war on anyone "tainted" with western ways. In an orgy of extermination, the Khmer Rouge killed as many as 1.5 million Cambodians—a quarter of the population. Many were shot, while the rest died from starvation, disease, or mistreatment in labor camps or on forced marches.

Vietnamese Occupation of Cambodia In 1978 the Vietnamese marched into Cambodia, bringing the slaughter to a halt. The aim of the invaders was not to stop the killing, however. Rather, they feared that Cambodia was interested in conquering

---

[3.] In the first six months of that year, more bombs were dropped on Cambodia then on Japan in all of World War II.

WITHDRAWAL AND AFTERMATH (1973 TO THE PRESENT)

parts of Vietnam that had once been part of the ancient Cambodian empire.

Since 1978, the Vietnamese have remained in Cambodia, battling three guerrilla factions. The fighting has created hundreds of thousands of new refugees, and Cambodia's agony continues. The military cost for Vietnam, meanwhile, is high. In addition to maintaining an army in Cambodia, Vietnam controls Laos and must defend its northern border against a hostile China. One of the world's twelve poorest countries, Vietnam maintains the fourth largest army. Such military energies and expenses also distract from the urgent problems that have faced the Vietnamese people since the Communist victory.

Vietnam Unified On July 2, 1976, a new national assembly proclaimed the official unification of Vietnam as the Socialist Republic of Vietnam. Hanoi was declared the capital, and in other ways the North ensured its domination over the South. All but one of the top offices in the new government went to former leaders of North Vietnam. The North Vietnamese flag, anthem, and emblem, meanwhile, were made the official symbols of Vietnam.

The unification of Vietnam and choice of official symbols, however, could not hide deep problems. Thirty years of war had left the country in ruin. More than 4 million Vietnamese soldiers and civilians had been killed or wounded, roughly 10 percent of the population. Huge areas of southern Vietnam, meanwhile, had been defoliated by American herbicides, leaving the land barren.[4] Ill-conceived economic plans—including one scheme to develop such heavy industries as steel and chemicals at the expense of agriculture—only made matters worse. Unable to raise capital, Vietnam's economic plans never took shape, and today Vietnam has virtually *no* industry. The most ordinary of goods—soap, stationery, needles—are impossible to find. Efforts to collective agriculture, in addition, harmed the nation's agriculture output. Food supplies remain far below the needs of the people, and most foods are rationed and expensive. Malnutrition is widespread.

"Re-education Camps" Many of the problems facing the Communist leadership have had to do with southern Vietnam. Soon after the 1975 victory, more than 400,000 South Vietnamese soldiers, civil servants, political activists, teachers, doctors, and lawyers were forced into **"re-education camps."** Most detainees

---

[4.] During the war, crews sprayed more than 100 million pounds of the chemical over millions of acres of forests, destroying an estimated one half of South Vietnam's timberlands.

have since been released, but thousands remain behind. Although Vietnam has avoided the blood-letting of Cambodia, human rights organizations have denounced the camps.

The Communist leaders have found, in any case, that "re-education" has not been a success. During the war, differences between the two parts of the country were sharpened, and Hanoi's heavy-handed methods have not ensured unification. Just as southern Vietnam resisted American influence in the 1960's, so too does it resist the North. Peasant opposition to collectivization, for instance, was so strong in southern Vietnam that the program was abandoned.

Changing Saigon's name to Ho Chi Minh City, meanwhile, has not stamped out that city's historic corruption. The black market still flourishes there, and bribery is necessary to get anything done. Corruption, in fact, seems to have spread throughout the country.

Soviet Backing To keep the economy afloat, Vietnam has had to turn to the Soviet Union. Some 6,000 Soviet advisers run an aid program ranging from $1 and $2 billion a year. Vietnam pays a heavy price for this aid. It is forced to provide the Soviet Union with raw materials, sinking it into a colonial relationship. Soviet aircraft and warships also use the former American complex at Camrahn Bay.

Most Vietnamese deeply resent the Russians, but they have nowhere else to turn. Border wars fought with China in 1979, 1980, and 1984 put an end to any notion of friendship with Vietnam's neighbor to the north. Establishing better relations with the United States has also proved difficult. The United States has been unhappy with Vietnam's ties with the Soviet Union and with its invasion of Cambodia. In addition, Americans have remained antagonistic because of Vietnam's seeming indifference to the fate of some 2,500 servicemen still listed as missing in action. Until the **MIA's** are accounted for, there seems to be little chance that the two countries will establish normal diplomatic relations.

Refugees from Indochina American public opinion has also remained hostile to the Communist government in Hanoi because of the agonizing spectacle of thousands of refugees fleeing Vietnam by boat. More than 1.5 million **boat people**, leaving behind all personal possessions in their determination to escape, have left Vietnam since 1975. As many as 50,000 of them have perished in flight, while many thousands of others find themselves in wretched refugee camps scattered throughout Southeast Asia. A million Vietnamese have found homes in other countries,

WITHDRAWAL AND AFTERMATH (1973 TO THE PRESENT)

including more than 750,000 who have settled in the United States. In addition to the Vietnamese refugees, some 125,000 Cambodians and 150,000 Laotians have fled their unhappy homelands and have made their way to the United States.

The United States and the Costs of Vietnam The influx of Asian refugees in recent years has helped play a part in focusing American attention and interest on the Vietnam War. In the years immediately following the American department from Vietnam, however, the nation as a whole seemed eager only to forget the war. Perhaps because the memories of Vietnam were so painful no one wanted to discuss it. As a result, there was no finger-pointing or angry debate over who "lost" Vietnam. By late 1975 a columnist wrote, "Americans have somehow blocked it out of their consciousness. They don't talk about it. They don't talk about its consequences."

The costs of Vietnam, nevertheless, were enormous. More than 58,000 Americans had been killed in Vietnam, while over 300,000 were wounded, half of them seriously. Because of the enemy's use of booby traps, mines, and ambushes, some 10,000 servicemen had lost at least one limb. Meanwhile, the financial costs were staggering. The United States paid at least $150 billion in direct expenses. Indirect expenses probably total at least that, while other costs—payments to veterans, interest on debts—continue to mount. Finally, the nation's political atmosphere was poisoned. Johnson had been denied a second term, Nixon had resigned in disgrace, and a wary public viewed the office of President with cynicism and suspicion.

Vietnam Veterans The primary victims of the nation's desire to forget Vietnam were those who had fought there. Upon their return home, many veterans experienced problems with drugs, alcohol, and joblessness. Thousands faced the uncertainty of health problems caused by exposure to a chemical herbicide called **Agent Orange**, which may cause cancer. As many as 700,000 veterans suffer from various forms of post-traumatic stress disorders, known to earlier generations as shell-shock or battle-fatigue.

The great majority of veterans, of course, adjusted well to civilian life. Still, they had to confront the public's suspicion that they were dangerous lunatics, ready to explode into violence. If an individual committed a crime and was then identified as a Vietnam vet, for instance, it invariably made headlines and re-enforced an unfair stereotype.

VIETNAM FACT

John Kerry, later a United States senator from Massachusetts, described the bewildering experience shared by many servicemen of being whisked home from Vietnam by jet, not to a ticker-tape parade but to a nation grown hostile to the war: "There I was, a week out of the jungle, flying home from San Francisco to New York. I fell asleep and woke up yelling, probably a nightmare. The other passengers moved away from me—a reaction I noticed more and more in the months ahead. The country didn't [care] about the guys coming back, or what they'd gone through. The feeling toward them was 'Stay away—don't contaminate us with whatever you've brought back from Vietnam.'"

A Changed View For many years the veterans felt a smoldering resentment at their lack of recognition. They watched as in 1977 one of Jimmy Carter's first official acts as President was to pardon all draft resisters from the Vietnam War period. Then, in 1981, the nation joyfully welcomed home a group of hostages held captive in Iran.

These actions, combined with the general public neglect, convinced the veterans that they must take action. They themselves made the plans that led to construction of the striking V-shaped Vietnam Veterans Memorial in Washington, D.C. Two million people a year now visit the memorial, gazing at the names of the more than 58,000 Americans killed or missing in action in Vietnam.

Meanwhile, the popular view of the Vietnam veterans has changed. Now they have become popular culture heroes, viewed as brave fighters who were let down by their government and nation. Suddenly, too, there was a torrent of books, films, and television programs dealing with the subject of Vietnam.

The Meaning of Vietnam If Americans were more willing to talk about Vietnam, they are unable to agree about its meaning. Most people would concur that there is a yearning to restore the United States to its old position in the world. Still, there is little backing in the country for a return to the 1960's style of global intervention. The memory of Vietnam continues to create

WITHDRAWAL AND AFTERMATH (1973 TO THE PRESENT)

strong opposition to American involvement in such trouble spots as Central America or the Middle East.

There continues to be sharp disagreement, moreover, about America's decision to fight in South Vietnam in the first place. There are those who argue that it was unnecessary, immoral, or impractical to fight in a region that was of little strategic importance to the United States or to have intervened in a civil war that did not concern the United States. Others see the United States' role as a selfless attempt to save a country from aggression—"in truth a noble war," as President Ronald Reagan has stated. They point to the events of recent years—particularly the flight of the boat people—as justification for American intervention.

The question of commitment, however, leads to a second issue: the reason for the American failure. There is no lack of second-guessing, with political leaders, military strategists, and the media all being blamed for America's first lost war. Of course, whether a stronger counterinsurgency program, or earlier bombing of the North, or a formal declaration of war, or the banning of the media—whether any of these would have made the slightest difference in the end can never be known. One fact remains clear: the Vietnam War marked a turning point in American history. Since the Vietnam War, most Americans have tried to adapt to the reality that there are limits to this nation's power and that those limits have to be considered in any foreign policy decision.

SECTION 2 REVIEW

1. **Vocabulary to Know** "re-education camp," MIA, boat people, Agent Orange

2. **People to Identify** Pol Pot

3. (a) What happened to Laos in 1975? (b) To Cambodia?

4. Name some of the problems that Vietnam has faced since unification.

5. Why have relations between the United States and Vietnam not improved?

6. What problems did many Vietnam veterans experience after their return home?

7. **Critical Thinking** What is your view of the main lesson to be learned from America's involvement in Vietnam?

CHAPTER 7 REVIEW

Vocabulary and People

Agent Orange
Bach Mai
boat people
Christmas bombings
convoy of tears
Gerald Ford
Hanoi Hilton
Graham Martin
MIA
Paris peace settlement
Pol Pot
"re-education camp"
War Powers Act

Identification

Write the numbered sentences on a sheet of paper. Fill in the blank in each sentence with one of these words: *MIA's, Paris peace settlement, War Powers Act.*

1. Under the terms of the _____, North Vietnamese troops were allowed to remain in South Vietnam.

2. Congress tried to curb the President's power in conducting foreign policy by passing the _____ in 1973.

3. Until the _____ are accounted for, relations between the United States and Vietnam are likely to remain poor.

Reviewing the Main Ideas

1. What problems did Thieu face in the days and months after the Paris peace settlement?

2. How did Congress restrict the options of American Presidents in Southeast Asia?

3. To what extent did the domino theory come true?

4. (a) What was the American attitude regarding Vietnam by 1975? (b) How can such an attitude be explained?

5. How has the American treatment of Vietnam veterans changed in recent years?

WITHDRAWAL AND AFTERMATH (1973 TO THE PRESENT)

Critical Thinking

Former Secretary of State Henry Kissinger made the following observation about the effect of the Vietnam War on the United States. Read what Kissinger had to say and then answer the questions that follow:

> Vietnam is still with us. It has created doubts about American judgment, about American credibility, about American power—not only at home, but throughout the world. It has poisoned our domestic debate. So we paid an exorbitant price for the decisions that were made in good faith and for good purpose.

1. What does Kissinger believe Vietnam has done to American credibility?

2. Does Kissinger seem to think that American motives in getting involved in Vietnam were good or bad?

3. In what way is Vietnam with us today? What recent crisis—domestic or foreign—has stirred up memories of Vietnam?

KEY DATES IN THE VIETNAM WAR

1950	(July 26) President Truman provides aid to French military in Indochina.
	(May 7) France loses the Battle of Dienbienphu.
1954	(August) Geneva Conference divides Vietnam at the 17th parallel pending a settlement to be reached through nationwide elections.
1955	United States begins to provide aid to South Vietnam.
1957	The Vietcong begin to rebel against the South Vietnamese government of Ngo Dinh Diem.
1961	President Kennedy increases the number of American military advisers to South Vietnam.
1963	(November 1) South Vietnamese generals overthrow the Diem government.
1964	(August 7) Congress passes the Gulf of Tonkin Resolution giving the President the authority to take "all necessary measures" and "to prevent further aggression."
1965	(February 6) United States begins sustained bombing of North Vietnam.
	(March 6) The first United States combat troops land at Danang, South Vietnam.
1967	American troop strength approaches 500,000.
1968	(January 30) The Communists launch the Tet offensive, a major campaign against South Vietnamese cities.
	(October 31) President Johnson halts the bombing of North Vietnam, providing the basis for negotiations.

KEY DATES IN THE VIETNAM WAR

1968   (May 10) Paris peace talks begin.

1969   (March 18) President Nixon begins the secret bombing of Cambodia.

1970   (February 20) Presidential adviser Henry Kissinger begins secret peace talks with the North Vietnamese.

(April 30) United States troops enter Cambodia to destroy Communist supply bases.

1972   (December 18) Christmas bombing of North Vietnam begins.

1973   (January 27) The United States, North and South Vietnam, and the Vietcong sign a cease-fire agreement.

(March 29) The last United States combat troops leave South Vietnam.

1975   (April 17) In Cambodia, Phnompenh falls to the Khmer Rouge.

(April 30) Saigon falls to Communist forces; South Vietnam surrenders.

1982   (November 11) Vietnam Veterans Memorial unveiled in Washington. D.C.

VIETNAM BIOGRAPHY

The Trung Sisters

The earliest Vietnamese heroes were those who resisted Chinese rule. Among the most revered is Trung Trac, the wife of an aristocrat executed after the first Vietnamese rebellion in A.D. 39. To avenge her husband's death, Trung Trac and her sister Trung Nhi, raised an army. For three years the **Trung sisters** were able to carve out their own independent kingdom, reaching south to Hué and north into southern China. Finally, one of China's best generals was sent to put down the revolt. Rather than accept the shame of surrender, the sisters threw themselves into a river and drowned.

The Trung uprising was a battle between two ruling classes—Chinese and Vietnamese—over who would rule Vietnam. Nevertheless, it is remembered in Vietnam today as the first blow for national independence.

Bao Dai

Once described as a "slippery-looking customer rather on the pudgy side and freshly dipped in Crisco," Vietnam's last emperor, **Bao Dai**, was a corrupt playboy but he was no fool. He knew above all how to adapt to his nation's ever-changing political scene.

Crowned emperor at the death of his father in 1925, when he was just twelve, Bao Dai spent the next seven years in Paris. When he returned home, he learned quickly that the French intended that he follow their orders. Allowed to remain on his imperial throne during the Japanese occupation, he next served for a year as Ho Chi Minh's "supreme adviser." Brought back to the throne by the French in 1949, he spent his last years in power avoiding responsibility while stealing from his fellow countrymen. A secret United States report revealed that by 1952 he was directly pocketing more than $4 million a year in American aid. Most of that money—about 5 percent of the regime's total revenues—was transferred immediately to French and Swiss banks.

By 1954, running low of funds to finance his extravagant lifestyle, Bao Dai sold control of the Saigon police to a mobster boss for $1 million. He finally met his match the next year when Ngo Dinh Diem, whom he had named to be prime minister, turned on him and forced his abdication. Bao Dai returned to France, where he had lived as a youth.

Madame Nhu

She was beautiful and she was opinionated, and if there was just one Vietnamese that the American public could identify in the early 1960's it was probably **Madame Nhu**. Born to a prominent Catholic family and educated in the North, the young Le Xuan, or Beautiful Spring, spoke only French and never learned to write in her native language. In later years, she would write out her speeches in French and then have them translated into Vietnamese.

Married in 1943 to Ngo Dinh Nhu, reputedly one of her mother's lovers, she moved with him to the southern town of Dalat, where he edited a newspaper. In 1955, following Diem's ouster of Bao Dai in the rigged election, the Nhus moved into the presidential palace. Madame Nhu quickly assumed the duties of First Lady of her bachelor brother-in-law, becoming the only woman in the inner circle of power.

In the last years of the Diem government, as its leading players turned inward and more reclusive, the vain Madame Nhu became more outspoken. Her ill-chosen comments only made things worse. About the Buddhist "barbecues," as she called them, she once said, "Let them burn, and we shall clap our hands." In addition to incurring the hatred of the Buddhist majority, she was scorned by the educated and professional classes for what they believed was her hypocritical antivice campaign. As the end approached, she became more and more shrill, seeing enemies everywhere. On an overseas speaking tour when her husband and brother-in-law were murdered, she took up exile in Europe, where she lives to this day.

Tri Quang

The militant leader of Vietnam's Buddhists, **Tri Quang** organized the protests that led to Diem's downfall. For the next years, he continued to play a potent role in South Vietnam's chaotic factional and religious conflicts. For all his abilities as an organizer, however, Tri Quang failed to develop a political program around which the South Vietnamese could rally. In 1966, when he led protests both against Prime Minister Ky and the United States, Tri Quang went too far. Ky arrested him while he was on a hunger strike, and the Buddhist movement never regained its former power. After the Communist takeover in 1975, Tri Quang was banished to a monastery.

ARVN Soldiers

They were poorly led by inadequately trained, class-conscious officers. Few had much idea of what they were fighting for. Pay was low, and assignments were usually to locations far from home. Meals consisted only of rice and dry fish and a very simple soup. Yet, despite all these obstacles, the ARVN soldiers responded with gritty courage and with an ability to endure pain and suffering without complaint.

In the early years of the fighting, relations between the ARVN forces and their American advisers was good. With the big American troop build-up, however, the ARVN was largely shunted aside, relegated to minor operations and population control, which fostered a sense of inferiority. By the late 1960's tensions between Americans and South Vietnamese had increased. Americans ridiculed the ARVN, joking that its mode of attack was best illustrated by the statue of a seated soldier in the National Military Cemetery. Because of Vietcong infiltration into ARVN ranks, moreover, Americans kept South Vietnamese military personnel off their major bases and refused to share the details of military operations with them.

Nguyen Cao Ky

Vice President during the Tet offensive, the flamboyant **Nguyen Cao Ky** held a number of high positions during the American years in Vietnam. With his flashy flying suit, bright purple scarf, and ivory-handled pistol, Ky was always in the news. For some, he was a bold, inspiring leader who, as commander of the air force, was distinguished by the raids he led against the North. For others, he was a devious, conniving show-off.

Ky first gained attention in 1964 when he threatened to bomb the headquarters of squabbling generals during Khanh's regime. By the next year, he and Nguyen Van Thieu had maneuvered themselves into power, with Ky becoming prime minister. As head of the South Vietnamese government, he immediately gained notoriety by declaring that Vietnam needed someone like Hitler to solve its problems. Although the Americans had a hard time taking him seriously, he did travel to Hawaii in 1966 for a highly publicized meeting with Lyndon Johnson. Encouraged by

Johnson's words of praise, Ky soon cracked down hard against the Buddhists. But the next year, after a backstage arrangement by the Armed Forces Council, Ky became Thieu's vice president, a position he retained until 1971 when Thieu forced him from power.

During the Communist offensive of 1975 Ky, with his usual bravado, urged a Saigon rally to "let the cowards run away with the Americans" and promised to defend the city. Soon after, he fled the city and made his way to California, where he operates a liquor store today.

Nguyen Thi Binh

Madame Binh burst on the world scene when she showed up in Paris in 1968 as head of the negotiating team for the National Liberation Front. Thought of at first only as a token negotiator, she proved to be an articulate and tough advocate of the Communist position.

Born to a middle-class family in Saigon, Nguyen Thi Binh became a radical opponent of foreign rule while a student. Arrested in 1951 at an anti-French demonstration, she was sentenced to three years in prison, where she was tortured. After the Geneva Accords of 1954, she married a doctor and moved to the countryside, where she joined the anti-Diem movement. Named to the NLF's central committee in 1962, she traveled around the world as its "roving ambassador," explaining the Communist position.

Although Madame Binh did not participate in all the Paris negotiations, she was frequently in the public eye, making speeches and giving interviews. After the war, she became the minister of education in Communist Vietnam.

Nguyen Van Thieu

Surprisingly, he began his career as a member of the Vietminh. For the American public, however, **Nguyen Van Thieu** is remembered as the staunchly anti-Communist president of South Vietnam, elected in 1967 and 1971.

Caught up in the anti-colonial sentiment that swept Vietnam after the French return to Indochina in 1945, the youthful Thieu briefly joined the Vietminh. Disliking its Communist tendencies, however, he left to enter a French-supported military academy. After graduation, he fought in several campaigns against Ho's forces. He also married a prominent Vietnamese Catholic and converted to Catholicism.

American military advisers regarded Thieu as a promising officer, and after the French defeat, they sent him to the United States for training. Upon his return home, he proved adept at the intrigue that marked Vietnamese politics. He became the military chief of state in 1965, and after outmaneuvering Nguyen Cao Ky in 1967, was elected president, a post he held until the Communist victory.

In his years as president, Thieu never gained great popularity. In some ways he resembled Diem, whom he had helped to overthrow in 1963: he was suspicious, fearful of opposition, and increasingly isolated. When the end came in 1975, he fled Saigon and eventually settled in Great Britain.

INDEX

This index includes references not only to the text but to the pictures (*p*) as well. Page numbers that are marked *n* refer to footnotes.

A

Abrams, Creighton, 111, 116
Abzug, Bella, 126
Acheson, Dean, 16, 101
Agent Orange, 143
Agnew, Spiro, 114, 120
agrovilles, 36
Ali, Muhammad, 85
Alvarez, Everett, 57, 134
Annam, 6, 7
Annamese mountains, 2
antiwar protests, 80, 81–82, 84–85, 113–114, 118–120, 123
Army of the Republic of Vietnam (ARVN), 41, 73, 77, 135, 152
assimilation policy, 6
attrition, 74

B

Bach Mai hospital, 133
Baez, Joan, 85
Ball, George, 59
Banmethuot, 136
Bao Dai, 17, 23, 28, 29, 31, 34, 35; biography of, 150–151
Bay of Pigs, 39
Bay Vien, 33
Béhaine, Pigneau de, 4
B-52's, 61, 65, 93, 93n, 103, 112
Bien Hoa, 55
Binh Gia, 59
Binh, Nguyen Thi; biography of, 153
Binh Xuyen, 33, 34
black Americans, and civil rights movement, 80; and service in Vietnam, 84, 124
boat people, 142–143
body counts, 75
bombing of North Vietnam, U.S. considers, 52–53, 59; following Gulf of Tonkin incident, 57; air war begins, 60–61, 62; costs of, 62; halted (late 1965), 65; halted (1968), 102; during 1972 offensive, 127; Christmas bombing, 133
Brezhnev, Leonid, 126
Buddhists, opposition to Diem, 44–46, 80, 151; fighting with Catholics, 58; protests against Thieu, 135
Buffalo, University of, 119n
Bundy, McGeorge, 60
Bundy, William, 58–59

C

Calley, William, 115, 115n
Cambodia, as part of French Indochina, 5; Communist bases in 110–111, 116; secret U.S. bombing of, 111–112; overthrow of Sihanouk, 117; invasion of, 118–119; protests against invasion of 118–120; falls to Khmer Rouge, 140; under Pol Pot, 140; Vietnamese occupation of, 140–141

INDEX

Cam Ne, 71
Camranh Bay, 66, 79, 95, 136
Cao Dai, 11, 33
Carter, Jimmy, 144
Catholics, in colonial Vietnam, 3–4; flee from North, 24–25; status in South Vietnam, 33, 44; fighting with Buddhists, 58; protests against Thieu, 135
central highlands, 2, 60, 92, 127, 136
Chicago, Democratic National Convention (1968), 108–109
China, early domination of Vietnam, 1, 2, 5; Nationalist troops sent to Vietnam, 14, 15; Communist take-over of, 16, 17; recognizes Ho Chi Minh, 16; and aid to Vietminh, 16; at Geneva Conference, 23; and border fighting with Vietnam, 141, 142
Cholon, 47
Christmas bombing, 133
Chu Lai, 74
civil rights movement, 80
Clifford, Clark, named Secretary of Defense (1968), 67; advice following Tet offensive, 99
cluster bombs, 61
coastal lowlands, 2
Cochinchina, 6, 7, 11, 15
Colby, William, 116
cold war, 16
collectivization, 25

Colson, Chuck, 125
Columbia University, 84
Committee for a Sane Nuclear Policy (SANE), 81
Constitution, 5
containment policy, 16, 39
Con Thien, 93
"credibility gap," 61
Cronkite, Walter, 98
Crosby, Stills, Nash, and Young, 120

D

Dai Viet, 3
Daley, Richard, 108, 109
Danang, 5, 63, 95, *p130*, 136
defoliants, 77, 143
De Gaulle, Charles, 12, 29
détente, 126
Diem, Ngo Dinh. *See* Ngo Dinh Diem
Dienbienphu, Battle of (1954), 19–20, 20–21, 93
domino theory, 21, 139
Donlon, Roger, 59
Doors, The, 86
Doumer, Paul, 7–8
doves, 81, 84, 85, 109
draft, 82–83, 101n, 134n
drugs, in colonial Vietnam, 7–8; and youth movement, 85–86; use by American troops of, 124
Dulles, John Foster, 23, 33

E

Ehrlichman, John, 125n
Eisenhower, Dwight D; and

INDEX

Dienbienphu crisis, 21; and domino theory, 21; and support for Diem, 32; and policy of massive retaliation, 40
election, U.S. presidential (1964), 54–55, 69; (1968), 100–101, 109; (1972), 132–133
Ellsberg, Daniel, 125
Eltinge, USNS General Le Roy, p50
Ely, Paul, 21
enclave theory, 73
"enemies list," 125–126
Eugénie, empress of France, 5
Europeans, in Vietnam, 3–4, 5

F

Faure, Edgar, 33
Flaming Dart, 60
flexible response, 40
Fonda, Jane, 85, 126
Ford, Gerald, 135, 137
Fulbright, J. William, 65
fragging, 124
France, starts colonies in Indochina, 5; colonial policy of, 6–9; justice system of, 7; economic policies of, 7–9; occupied by Germany in World War II, 11; collaboration in Indochina with Japanese, 11; returns to Cochinchina, 15; recognizes Vietnamese independence (1946), 15; and Indochinese War, 15, 17–21; internal domestic problems of, 16; and Battle of Dienbienphu, 19–20, 21; at Geneva Conference, 22–25; leaves Vietnam, 33
French Foreign Legion, 14, 20, 21

G

Geneva accords, 24, 32, 41
Geneva Conference, 22–24, 32
genocide, 66
Gia-Long, 3
Giap, Vo Nguyen, 12, 17, 19–20, 92
Goldwater, Barry, 54, 69
Goodell, Charles, 113
Grateful Dead, 86
Great Britain, 14, 16
Great Society, 51, 52
Green Berets, 40, 56, 59
Green Berets (movie), 86n
Gregory, Dick, 126
Gruening, Ernest, 57
guerrilla warfare, 17–18, 40, 72–73, 76
Gulf of Tonkin, 56
Gulf of Tonkin Resolution, 57–58

H

Haight-Ashbury (San Francisco), 85
Haiphong, v, 15, 59, 62, 127
"Hamburger Hill," 115–116
Hanoi, 13, 15, 62, 127, 133
Harrington, Myron, 91

INDEX

hawks, 81, 86n, 113
helicopters, 43, 77
Hendrix, Jimi, 86
Herrick, John, 56
Hickel, Walter, 118
Hoa Hao, 12, 33
Ho Chi Minh, early life, 9; at Versailles Conference, 10; founds Indochinese Communist Party, 10; in Soviet Union and China, 10; anti-Japanese policy of, 11; forms Vietminh, 11; declares Vietnamese independence, 13; invites France back to Vietnam, 15; government of recognized by China and Soviet Union, 16; and fight against France, 17–18; and campaign against South Vietnam, 38, 53; orders start of Tet offensive, 94; death of, 113
Ho Chi Minh City (Saigon), 142
Ho Chi Minh Trail, 41, 53, 65, 122, 139
Hongay coal mines, 8
Hope, Bob, 78
Hué, v, 3, 35, 44; during Tet offensive, 91, 95–96, 115; evacuated during final offensive, 136
Humphrey, Hubert, 596, 108–109
Hunt, E. Howard, 125
Huston Plan, 120

I

Ia Drang Valley, 65

imperialism, 6
Indochinese Communist Party, 10

J

Jackson, Henry, 100
Jackson State College, 119n
Japan, occupies Indochina, 11–12; defeated in World War II, 12
Jefferson Airplane, 86
Johnson, Harold, 96
Johnson, Lady Bird, 89
Johnson, Lyndon B., and Dienbienphu crisis, 20; on Diem, 32; visit to South Vietnam (1961), 41; becomes President, 51; and Great Society, 51, 52; in election of 1964, 54–55; and Gulf of Tonkin Resolution, 55–58; considers deep involvement, 58–59, *p70*; avoids difficult decisions, 59, 99–100; approves beginning of air war, 60; and "credibility gap," 61; approves of U.S. combat troops in South Vietnam, 63; responds to antiwar movement, 85; withdraws from 1968 presidential race, *p90*, 102, 143; reaction to Tet, 96, 98–100; in 1968 presidential primaries, 100–101
Joplin, Janis, 86

INDEX

K

Kennan, George, 16
Kennedy, Edward, 126
Kennedy, John F., as Senator, 34; becomes President, 39; Cabinet officers and advisers of, 40; and Green Berets, 40; sends advisers to Vietnam, 41, 42; and public opinion, 42; and plot against Diem, 46–47, 126; assassinated, 51
Kennedy, Robert, 42, 54, 54n, 67, 100, 108
Kent State University, 119–120
Kerry, John, 144
Khanh, Nguyen, 52, 53–54, 64
Khe Sanh, 93, 94
Khmer Rouge, 117, 140
Khrushchev, Nikita, 39
King, Martin Luther, Jr., 85
Kissinger, Henry, 110, 121, 126, 132, 133, 147
Korean War, 16, 21, 22, 66, 81, 103
Kosygin, Aleksei, 60, 61
Krulak, Victor, 73
Ky, Nguyen Cao, becomes prime minister (1965), 64; departs South Vietnam, 138; biography of, 152–153

L

Laird, Melvin, 113, 134n
Laos, as part of French Indochina, 5; neutralist government established in, 39n; South Vietnamese invasion of, 112; U.S. bombing of, 139; falls to Communists, 139–140
Leclerc, Jacques Philippe, 15
Le Duc Tho, 121, 132, 133
LeMay, Curtis, 52–53, 59, 129
Liddy, G. Gordon, 125
Life magazine, 115
Lodge, Henry Cabot, named ambassador, 45; and coup plans, 46–47; seeks Republican nomination (1964), 54
Lon Nol, 117, 118, 140

M

MacArthur, Douglas, 12, 14, 42
McCarthy, Eugene, 100–101
McCarthy, Joseph, 51
McGovern, George, 127, 132
McKinley, William, 55
McNamara, Robert S.; named Secretary of Defense, 40; optimistic views of, 42; and debate over U.S. involvement, 42; advice to Johnson (1964), 52; accompanies Khanh, 53–54; calls for bombing halt (1965), 65; disillusionment with war (1967), 66; leaves office, 66–67; and Pentagon Papers, 125
Maddox, 56, 57
Mailer, Norman, 85

INDEX

Manchester, William, 86
Mansfield, Mike, 49
Mao Zedong, 16, 17
Marie Antoinette, 4
Martin, Graham, 137
massive retaliation, 40
Mekong Delta, 2, 127
Mekong River, 2
Mèndes-France, Pierre, 22–24
Mexican War, 81
MIA's (missing in action), 142
Minh, Duong Van, and 1963 coup plans, 46, 47; overthrown (1965), 52; head of state (1975), 138
Minh Mang, 4
missionaries (Christian), in Vietnam, 3–5; growing power of, 4; persecution of, 4
Mondale, Walter, 126
Monterey (California) rock festival, 86
moritoriums, 114
Morrison, Norman, 80
Morse, Wayne, 57, 57n
M16 rifle, 64
Muskie, Edmund, 126
Mylai massacre, 114–115, 123

N

Namath, Joe, 126
Nam Dong, 59
Nam-Viet, 3
napalm, 61
Napoleon III, 5
nationalism, 9
National Liberation Front (NLF), 35, 153
Navarre, Henri, 18–19
New Hampshire, presidential primary, 100–101
"New Left," 81, 84
Newsweek magazine, 80, 119
New York Times, 86, 125
Ngo Dinh Can, 35
Ngo Dinh Diem, background of, *p30*, 31, 34; defeats private armies, 33; forces abdication of Bao Dai, 34; campaign against Communists, 34–35; visits United States, 35; and power of family, 35; domestic opposition to, 36–37, 44–45, 46; and American anxiety over, 37, 46; declares martial law, 45; overthrown, 47 assassinated, 47
Ngo Dinh Luyen, 35
Ngo Dinh Nhu, 35–36, 45, 46, 47
Ngo Dinh Thuc, 35
Nguyen Canh, 4
Nguyen Ngoc Loan, 96
Nguyen Van Hinh, 33
Nhu, Madame, 35, 37, 44, 46; biography of, 151
Nixon, Richard M., and Dienbienphu crisis, 20; background of, 108; wins 1968 election, 109; and foreign policy, 109–110, 126; Vietnam strategy of, 110; and domestic dissent, 114, 120, 125; orders invasion of Cambodia,

160

INDEX

117–118; orders cease-fire (1970), 121–122; following invasion of Laos, 123; and détente policy, 126; and Watergate, 126, 135; re-elected, 132–133; orders Christmas bombing, 133; greets POW's, 134; assures Thieu of U.S. backing, 134; resigns, 135, 143
Nolting, Frederick, 37, 44, 45
northern highlands, 2
North Vietnam, and problems after partition, 25–26; strategy of (1965), 53; response to U.S. bombing of, 62; response to U.S. troop build-up in South, 75; plans Tet offensive, 92; and 1972 invasion of South, 126–127; and final offensive, 135–136

P

pacification, 77
Paris peace conference, begins, 103, 153; continues, 113; settlement reached, 133–134
partition of Vietnam (1954), 23–24
Pathet Lao, 139
Pentagon Papers, 125
Percival, John, 5
Pétain, Marshal, 11
Philippines, 4, 12, 74
Phnompenh, 117, 140
Phoenix program, 116

Phuoc Binh, 135
Pleiku, v, 60, 63
Pol Pot, 140
Portuguese, in Vietnam, 3
Potsdam Conference, 14
POW's (prisoners of war), 134
public opinion, U.S., in early 1960's, 42, 61; during mid-1960's, 80–87; following Tet offensive, 97, 98; following Cambodian invasion, 118–120; following Laotian invasion, 123; concerning fall of South Vietnam, 136–137, 143, 144–145

Q

Quang Duc, 44
Quangtri, 127, 136

R

Raye, Martha, 78
Reagan, Ronald, 145
Redding, Otis, 86
Red River Delta, 2, 3
refugees, 24–25, 97, 136–138, 141, 142–143
rice, cultivation of, 3, 8
Ridgway, Matthew, 21
rock music, 85–86
Rolling Thunder, 61
Romney, George, 108n
Rostow, Walt, 40, 59
rubber, 8

INDEX

S

Saigon, taken by French (1859), 5; return of French to, 14; Diem government in, 31, 32, 33, 34; reaction to Diem overthrow, 47; instability in, after Diem, 52, 58, 64; unpopularity of government in, 73, 97; attacked during Tet offensive, 95, 96; reaction to failed invasion of Laos, 123; refugee problem, 135; falls to Communists, 137–138; named changed, 142
Schoenbrun, David, 17
search and destroy strategy, 72
Scranton, William, 120
Selective Service System, 82. *See also* draft
Selma (Alabama), 80
seventeenth parallel, 24, 60
Sihanouk, Prince Norodom, 111, 117
"silent majority," 114
South China Sea, 2
South Koreans, in Vietnam, 74
South Vietnam, established, 32; after fall of Diem, 52, 58, 64; and Vietnamization, 112; following departure of U.S., 135; falls to Communists, 135–138
Soviet Union, and cold war, 16; recognizes Ho Chi Minh, 16; at Geneva Conference, 23–24; aid to North Vietnam, 60, 61; and backing of postwar Vietnam, 142
Spanish, in Vietnam, 3, 5; in Philippines, 4
Spellman, Francis Cardinal, 34
Spock, Benjamin, 85
Stennis, John, 100
strategic hamlets, 36
Students for a Democratic Society (SDS), 81

T

Taylor, Maxwell, 40, 41, 53, 58, 59, 60, 63
Tchepone (Laos), 122
television, and coverage of war, 71, 95, 97, 105
Tet offensive (1968), 91–98
Tet '69, 110
Thailand, 74
Thieu, Nguyen Van, becomes chief of state (1965), 64; meets Nixon, 112–113; mistrust of peace settlement, 134; following withdrawal of U.S., 135; final days of leadership, 136–137; departs South Vietnam, 138; biography of, 153–154
Time magazine, 81
Tri Quang; biography of, 151
Tonkin, 6, 7
Truman, Harry S., 16–17, 51, 55
Trung sisters; biography of, 150

INDEX

Turner Joy, 56

U

United States, and aid to Vietminh during World War II, 12; and Vietnamese independence, 13; and cold war, 16; and aid to France, 17; recognizes Bao Dai, 17; and Dienbienphu crisis, 21; at Geneva Conference, 23; and backing for Diem, 31, 32, 33, 39; concern over Diem regime, 38–39; advisers in South Vietnam, 41, 42; and overthrow of Diem, 46, 47; policy toward South Vietnam (1964), 53–54; covert attacks against North, 56; and Gulf of Tonkin incident, 56–57; begins bombing North, 57, 61–62, *p106*; sends combat troops to South Vietnam, 62; and home front, 71–72, 80–87; early strategy of, 72–74; measures progress of war, 75; faces guerrilla warfare, 76–77; and logistical achievements, 77–78; and efforts to boost morale, 78–79; fears another Dienbienphu, 93; and Tet offensive, 94–98; and Nixon strategy to end war, 110; invades Cambodia, 117–118; problems of troop morale, 125–126; and Indochinese refugees, 142–143; and costs of Vietnam, 143; and Vietnam veterans, 143; and meaning of Vietnam, 144–145

U.S. Army Special Forces. *See* Green Berets

U.S. Office of Strategic Services (OSS), 12

V

Versailles, French court at, 4; conference ending World War I, 9–10

Vietcong, founded, 35; terror campaign of, 38–39, 103; in Battle of Chu Lai, 74; and guerrilla warfare, 75; and Tet offensive, 95, 97; and 1972 offensive, 127

Vietminh, founded, 11; cooperates with United States during World War II, 12; uprising against French in Saigon, 14; war with France, 15–16, 17–21; and Geneva Conference, 23–24; militants move north, 24

Vietnam, map of, vi; geography of, 2–3; during World War II, 11–13; and war between France and Vietminh, 17–21; divided at Geneva Conference, 23–24, 32; unified (1976), 138, 141; occupies Cambodia (1978), 140–141; current problems facing, 141–142; "re-education"

163

INDEX

camps in, 141–142; Soviet backing of, 142
Vietnam Independence League. *See* Vietminh
Vietnamization, 112
Vietnam veterans, 143–144
Vietnam Veterans Memorial, v, 144
Vuong Van Dong, 38

W

Walker Commission, 109
Wallace, George, 109
War Powers Act, 134
Watergate, v, 125n, 126, 134
Wayne, John, 78, 86n
Westmoreland, William, named U.S. commander in South Vietnam, 54; requests combat troops (1965), 62–63; optimism of, 67; strategy of, 72–74; anticipates Tet offensive, 94; and troop requests after Tet, 98–99; on impact of Tet, 105; replaced, 111
Wheeler, Earle, 94
Wilson, Woodrow, 9–10, 55
Women's Strike for Peace, 81
Woodstock, 86
World War I, 9, 72, 103
World War II, 11–13, 14, 16, 72, 103

X

Xuanloc, 137
Xuan Thuy, 113

Y

youth movement, 85–86

Z

Zhou Enlai, 23, 126

164

#33-91